ZERO TO HOME OWNER IN 8 SIMPLE STEPS

A FIRST TIME HOME BUYER'S GUIDE TO SKIP THE STRESS, AVOID COSTLY MISTAKES, AND SAVE THOUSANDS

SAM LOVELESS

CONTENTS

INTRODUCTION

"Oh, and here's your house key!" As my agent handed me the key to my first home, I couldn't believe I was actually a homeowner. Having moved from a basement apartment with a low ceiling, I remember wandering around my new home and gawking at its relative roominess. The process had been swift, with very few hiccups, but I'll never forget that feeling of relief and excitement once the deal was officially complete.

I'm sure, dear reader, you are looking for a similar outcome, and I'm delighted to tell you that you've come to the right place. The reason my first-time home buying process went so smoothly is because, as it so happens, I am formally trained in housing and personal finance and have educated hundreds of clients to secure homeownership. And I'm happy to tell you that you don't need a graduate degree like me in order to have a smooth process yourself. In fact, by reading this book, you have everything you need at your fingertips. Not only will your home buying process be smoother, but you will also save thousands of dollars, cut down your time from start to finish, and save yourself the massive headache that unprepared home buyers accept as "just part of the process."

You may be asking yourself if the information in this book will suit you in your situation, and while there are some unique borderline scenarios, this book will be immensely helpful to the vast majority of U.S. homebuyers, no matter what point they are in the process. The aim of this book is to give you a succinct yet thorough understanding of the home buying process. It will provide you with every detail you'll need to know to go from having absolutely no inkling as to how purchasing a home works, to reclining in your new living room, confident you've gotten the best deal possible. Not only that, I want you to be able to stay in your home as long as you'd like without worrying that you've bitten off more than you could chew. That will start with creating a solid financial foundation and by making crucial, wise choices as you go through the process.

In this book, I will first give you a brief overview of the entire process so you will be able to orient yourself within each step. I'll help you come up with your own game plan so you'll be confident that this is the best choice for your situation. I'll also teach you how to connect with the professionals you'll need, as well as how to save money doing it. By the end of this book, you'll understand when and how each element should be completed, along with an idea of typical costs and timeframes. The best part is the time and money you'll save by following my tips throughout the book. I know all about the typical mistakes and problems experienced by first-time home buyers, and I want to help you avoid them.

This brings me to you. If I might venture a guess, I would suppose that you are currently stressed out *and* excited. Such a unique mix of opposing emotions! The idea of homeownership may just be a twinkle in your eye; or perhaps you're mid-way through your process, having a panic attack because you can't remember if you were supposed to set up the appraisal, and what if the home inspector finds a problem, and what happens to your earnest money, and were you supposed to bring cookies for everyone at closing??? First of all, don't bother bringing cookies unless an overwhelming love for baking compels you. Second, take a nice, deep breath. I've got you covered. I am prone to overstressing myself, but trust me, this process is not nearly as scary as you think it is. And by reading this book, you will be setting yourself up for not only stable, long-term homeownership, but a secure financial foundation upon which wealth-building can begin in earnest.

You may be asking yourself, who is this Sam Loveless, and what gives her the right to tell me to calm down? Good question! You know those people who get so obsessed with something, they just won't shut up about it? And you're like, "Whoa, I think you need to find some new hobbies." Well, I am obsessed with homes. No joke, my favorite time of year is my local Parade of Homes where I get to drag my husband across our county, walking through a dozen homes, picking up some useless swag, and formulating my perfect dream house. I check my local market nearly every day, even when I'm not looking to actually purchase a home. I can't help it, I just love everything about homes!

But aside from my perhaps unhealthy obsession, I also happen to have degrees and certifications from esteemed universities and institutions. Way back in the day, I took a personal finance college course, and it changed my life. What a novel idea that you could accumulate wealth and find financial stability on any income if you just learned the tools they *should* have taught us all in high school. Long story short, I graduated magna cum laude, college valedictorian with straight A's (except for one A minus that I don't want to talk about), and I loved it so much, I went on to pursue a graduate degree. While working on my master's, I was employed by my university to educate students and the public about everything from basic budgeting to investing for retirement, and of course, the homebuying process. I still remember the dank basement of a local bank where we would teach an 8-hour long workshop for community members, bringing in various real estate professionals to present, and helping our students work toward stable homeownership. (Don't even worry, we always brought donuts and juice for sustenance.) I was also flown all over the country for various housing and financial counseling workshops and conventions, published several articles including my master's thesis on homeownership, and completed numerous certifications in that field.

All that to say: I love homes. And I have a passion for personal finance. Homeownership is certainly not for everyone, but I believe anyone can learn this process and prepare themselves to be financially home-ready. While this book devotes only one chapter to that financial foundation, just know that it is a critical component for secure, long-term homeownership. This book will focus on the home buying process as a whole, and I will give you valuable tips and tricks along the way. I can't even tell you how glad I am you're here. You're going to be ecstatic that you decided to read it, both in the short-term, and years in the future when you're comfortably building your wealth and chilling in your beautiful home.

So without further ado, let's hop into it!

1

UNDERSTAND THE BIG PICTURE: A STEP-BY-STEP CHEAT SHEET SO NOTHING FALLS THROUGH THE CRACKS

I magine pouring out a ten-thousand piece puzzle onto your table. Your task is to complete the puzzle as quickly as you can, but there's a big problem: there's no picture available of what the finished image will be. You see dozens of green pieces, red ones, maybe that one is supposed to be part of a sky? Does this sound like a fun activity? What if you had to complete it on a deadline and you might lose thousands of dollars if you don't? Do you think you might get a little lost and stressed out? I sure would!

Well, going through the home buying process can induce similar anxiety, if you don't understand the big picture. You may know that at some point you'll need an appraisal, but you don't know when it happens, who orders it, and if it needs to happen before or after a home inspection. Just as you need to see the picture on the puzzle box to understand how each piece is supposed to fit together and what you're aiming for, so, too, is it helpful to get the 20,000-foot view of the home buying process.

This chapter will be brief and is intended to help you see how each piece of the process fits together, and in what order, so that as we dive more deeply into each step in subsequent chapters, you'll be able to orient yourself. Think of it as your quick-reference guide, and know that we will get into the details and money-saving tips later.

The bedrock of this process is based on the assumption that you have already weighed the pros and cons of homeownership and are ready to at least learn about the process itself. You may still be on the fence, and if that's you, I'm so glad you're here! This will be helpful in making your decision. And if you've already embarked, buckle up and prepare to save time and money!

So while I won't be getting into the pros and cons of homeownership specifically, I will say that buying a home is a big decision, and one not to be taken lightly. Everyone's circumstances are unique, and ultimately, it's going to be up to you (and any co-signer) to decide if it's right for you. Yes, homeownership comes with many, many benefits, but it truly isn't right for everyone. And if that's you? That's okay. It doesn't mean it won't be right for you in the future. This book will provide you with the information you need to determine that for yourself.

So, let's hop to it and dive into your "Quick Reference Guide." Come back here if you get lost or if you find the zoomed-out view helpful. You may also want to refer to this chapter once you've finished the book and need to just pop in for a quick reminder. I'm hoping that this will help you feel less overwhelmed by clearing up the big picture and giving you a peek at that puzzle picture for which you'll be aiming.

8-Step Quick Reference Guide

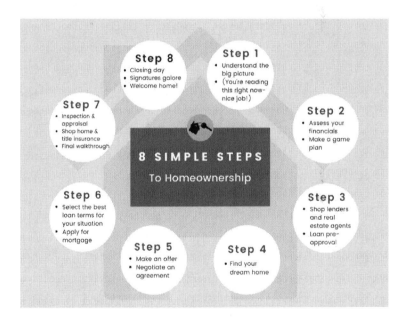

STEP 1: UNDERSTAND THE BIG PICTURE

- Approximate time: 10-20 minutes
- Approximate cost: $0.00

This is what you're doing by reading this chapter, and you should pat yourself on the back for doing a good job! This step will only take a few minutes of your time to complete and you're basically halfway done already. Step 1 paves the way for you to succeed in all the other steps, so feel free to take notes and highlight along the way.

STEP 2: ASSESS YOUR FINANCIAL SITUATION AND MAKE A GAME PLAN

- Approximate time: 1 to 8 weeks
- Approximate cost: $0.00 to $30.00

This is not a step you'll want to skip, especially if you intend to stay in a home long-term. Your financials are the foundation upon which all else is built, so we'll want to make sure you're building on sturdy ground. Completing this step will allow you to feel confident going forward, knowing that you are thoroughly prepared for any situation. It will also set you up for the best possible loan terms, which can shave thousands of dollars off your total costs. We will be covering the following items in detail inside chapter two.

In step 2, you will:

- Evaluate your current spending and budget. (Don't worry; if you've never budgeted before, I've got some resources for you.)
- Make a hypothetical "post-purchase" budget to help you determine how much you can actually afford. (Your lender will likely come up with a different number.)
- Calculate how much money you'll need to save for a down payment and other costs.
- Calculate your Debt to Income Ratio (DTI) and pay off any necessary debts.
- Pull your credit report and make sure it's good enough to get you an optimal loan rate. (Anything over 720 should be great, but below that will likely lead to less favorable loan terms, which translates into higher costs for you). Correct any mistakes with the three credit bureaus, and make any possible improvements to your score.
- Look into first-time homebuyer programs in your area to see if you qualify for any financial assistance, sweat equity, etc.

These foundational items have a lot of potential to save you money and strengthen your financial health regardless of whether you go through with a home purchase or not, so I hope you take this step as slowly as you need to set yourself up for success!

STEP 3: SHOP LENDERS AND REAL ESTATE AGENTS, AND APPLY FOR LOAN PRE-APPROVAL

- Approximate time: 3-30 days
- Approximate cost: $0

The main message from this step is an emphatic, "shop around!" Your lender and your agent can be hired in any order or simultaneously, but it is important that you find a good fit on both counts. Doing so will save you so much time and money, it's not even funny.

In step 3 you will:

- Shop around for the best lender, pitting several against each other to negotiate the most favorable terms for yourself
- Find and hire a buyer's real estate agent. It technically won't cost you anything, and the benefit they will provide you is enormous
- Skip the real estate attorney unless you've got a crazy property situation
- Get a pre-approval letter from your chosen lender

(we'll learn about different loan types and their considerations in step 6)

STEP 4: FIND THE PERFECT HOME

- Approximate time: 5-50 days
- Approximate cost: $0

This is the best part, in my opinion. As usual, take your time if you can, and really brainstorm all your needs and wants, present and future. Search for only homes you can afford, consider relevant factors, and avoid decision paralysis.

In step 4 you will:

- Evaluate which type of home will work best for you
- Come up with a list of needs and wants for your new home and prioritize them
- Use websites and your real estate agent to search for matching homes
- Tour a reasonable number of homes in person
- Evaluate which specific property will work best for you

STEP 5: MAKE AN OFFER THAT WILL LET YOU SLEEP AT NIGHT

- Approximate time: 1-14 days
- Approximate cost: $1000-$5000 in earnest money (will likely go toward your closing costs once the process is finished)

You've found the home of your dreams and you're ready to pull the trigger! Are you so excited? Nervous? This step can have relatively variable costs and timeframes, depending on your area, the market, and your seller. Your real estate agent will be your main resource here, so you'll be relying on her heavily. Be sure to understand everything you sign, and be sure to really commit if you're ready to move ahead.

In this step you will:

- Craft an offer with your real estate agent, considering your budget, home repairs, and whether the current market is favoring sellers or buyers
- Include any and all necessary contingencies in your offer (inspection, appraisal, financing, title, etc.)
- Decide how much earnest money to offer
- Get as many seller concessions as you can, considering the market

- Submit your offer, which includes your estimated closing date
- Negotiate with the seller's agent (through your buyer's agent) until a deal has been accepted by both parties. Hooray!

STEP 6: APPLY FOR YOUR MORTGAGE

- Approximate time: 30 days
- Approximate cost: $0 for now (you'll pay at closing)

If you've followed all previous steps, this one will be a breeze. You should already have all your needed documentation and paperwork at hand, so you'll just be handing those over to your lender, along with anything else she requires from you. In this step, you'll be learning about various types of loans and how to decide which will suit you best. You'll also learn more about your payment and the best practices to speed the process along and save money. The concepts in this step are perhaps the most important when it comes to overall money-saving, so pay close attention and consider implementing my tips along the way.

In this step you will:

- Deliver all paperwork to your lender
- Learn what credit score will be acceptable and how it's used when a spouse will be co-signing with you

- Consider your credit score, down payment, and debt-to-income ratio (DTI), and then pick the loan type that is best for you (FHA, USDA, VA, Conventional)
- Pick the most advantageous loan term and learn about the pros and cons of 15-year and 30-year mortgages
- Discover how to remove private mortgage insurance (PMI) early
- Negotiate any closing costs that you can, and learn what to expect
- Learn about PITI (principal, interest, taxes, insurance) and how taxes and insurance will be paid
- Avoid any large financial transactions during loan processing to reduce the chance of time delays
- Save literally tens of thousands of dollars by making extra payments to your mortgage. This is my very favorite part, so buckle up!

STEP 7: INSPECTION, INSURANCE, AND APPRAISAL

STEP 8: CLOSING

2

ASSESS YOUR FINANCIALS: RELIEVE YOUR STRESS WITH AN AIR-TIGHT GAME PLAN

D id you ever hear where the wise man built his house? Even if you're unfamiliar with this adage, most people will recognize that it's probably a better idea to build a house on a rock rather than the sand. And yet, so many first-time homebuyers (or even seasoned homebuyers) overlook the most important part of purchasing their homes: their financial foundation. While every step of this process is crucial to understand, it will all be for nothing if you're not starting with a solid foundation. There are many aspects to a "firm financial foundation," but in this chapter, I'll be highlighting what I see as the most important and those that will ultimately spare you a thousand headaches down the road. The last thing I want is for you to realize your payment is unsustainable after you've already signed your closing documents. Taking each step in this chapter seriously will give you optimal loan terms, prepare you for life's financial hiccups, and set you up for long-term success. I wish I could reach through this book, look you in the eyes and say, "No seriously—this will change your life! Please just do it!"

One of the most common questions I've received from potential homeowners is, "how much house can I afford?" And it's an excellent question, to be sure. You'd hate to be touring mansions only to realize you can only afford a shack. The thing is, it's actually kind of a subjective matter. Can you "afford" the Big Mac, or should you settle for something less tasty from the value menu? You might *have* the money for whatever you want, but would it be wise to pick the most expensive? Only you can know for sure. That's all to say, there are several calculators and opinions on the matter, but ultimately, you know your budget, your habits, and your situation better than anyone else. Your lender will tell you that you qualify for a certain amount, but she doesn't really know what you can actually *afford*.

So, how can you determine for yourself what you can afford? Well, those online calculators aren't a bad place to start, but we'll be taking it a step further. You can google "how much house can I afford calculator" where you'll be presented with a plethora of options, and each will output a slightly different number. I'd advise checking some out just to give yourself a ballpark idea of a monthly mortgage payment to expect, and what price of home that would lend you. One of my favorite calculators is Dave Ramsey's, but keep in mind it's one of the more conservative ones. (Check the resource list at the end of this book for a hyperlink to his calculator.)

Whatever calculators you check out, here's the basic premise (and don't worry, I'll provide an example in just a bit). Take your net monthly take-home pay and multiply it by .25. This is basically 25% of your income, and ideally your monthly mortgage payment won't go above that. There are no policemen who will come and arrest you if you go over that number, but a great deal of research has indicated that homeowners who take on a monthly loan payment higher than this are more likely to experience a financial burden and end up in foreclosure (where the bank takes the home back and kicks you out). You can avoid that by refusing any loan that is more than a quarter of your income, possibly even 35% if you really feel your circumstances would allow for it, and be mindful that every dollar above that is increasing your risk for trouble.

Now for that quick example I promised. Let's say your take-home pay is $3,000 per month. Multiplying $3,000 by .25 gives you $750. This means that you ideally shouldn't pay more than about $750 per month for your mortgage payment. (This is total mortgage payment, including taxes and insurance, but we'll get to that in step 6.) I'll stress again that this choice is, of course, entirely up to you, and it may be that your situation would allow you to go above this amount. Perhaps you have a lot of other assets or you're already used to paying a certain amount for rent. Only you can know for sure what a wise loan size is, but I have some more tips coming up that will help guide your decision.

Once you have a monthly payment amount ballparked from either the simple calculation above or by running a few free, online calculators, this is the number you will use to calculate a general idea for your loan amount. Note that I say general idea, and that's because there are other factors to be considered, such as your down payment, interest rate, and what type of loan you get. We'll get into those in step 6, but keep in mind that most of these online calculators will do this work for you by factoring in these other variables. Instead of giving you the calculations here, I'll put some of my favorites in the resource section at the end for you to look into, as that will be a far better use of your time.

So let's say our $750 mortgage payment equates to a home priced at $138,000, based on the calculator's output. I have assumed a $750 payment, a down payment of $10,000, a loan term of 30 years, an interest rate of 3%, annual taxes of $2,000, and annual insurance of $520. (Please note that many of these factors can vary widely depending on your locale.).

Hopefully, this gives you a general idea of how to get your estimated mortgage payment and house price, but we're not done yet. As I mentioned, everything thus far has been to simply give you an idea of where to start. Ultimately, what really matters is your budget and whether or not that payment can fit comfortably within it.

YOUR BUDGET

I hear you over there groaning. Trust me, this doesn't have to be terrible. In fact, you don't even have to be a raging nerd like me to actually enjoy yourself! You may be relieved when I tell you that I'm not going to dive too deeply into various budgeting methods, but just know that if you've tried and failed budgeting before, there's another technique that will resonate with you much better. Your budget doesn't have to look like someone else's to be workable for you. As someone who has taught and tried virtually every budgeting technique out there, I can tell you that "jotting things down on a crumpled up piece of paper" works just fine for some folks. I'm not here to judge your technique (or lack thereof), I'm just here to tell you that making and keeping a budget will help you immensely in the acquisition and maintenance of your home, as well as your long-term financial health and wealth.

If you have no idea where to start, check out mint.com, everydollar.com, Google the envelope method, search YouTube and blogs for free Excel spreadsheet templates, or get yourself some basic sticky notes and a pen you like. There's no need to overcomplicate this. You're basically just keeping a log of all incoming money and outgoing money. That's it. However you want to do that, just get it done. The best budget is the one that you'll stick with, and stable homeownership requires a well-maintained budget. Also keep in mind that your budget may evolve with you as your finances evolve. That's not only ok, I'd say that's natural and necessary.

A few quick words to the beginner budgeters. Let's say you've never even attempted an actual budget. Hey, friend, no big deal; there's no better time than the present. Start by writing down every dime you spend for one month, and what you spend it on. You can categorize it as you go if you want, but it really doesn't need to be anything more than this. At the end of the month, look over your expenditures and add them all up. Were they more than you brought in that month? You'll likely be very surprised how much you actually spend, especially on food (that one gets me every time). I highly suggest doing this for at least a month before moving ahead with your home purchasing process. You need to have at least some idea of your current financial situation before taking on such a large financial obligation. Using the information you've gathered, you can decide what a reasonable amount to shoot for would be for each category going forward. You can pick as many or as few categories as would be helpful to you.

Whatever method you use, there are several components that will be very helpful to include, if you so choose. If you have any debts, include the monthly payment in your budget. I advised clients to have a separate document detailing their total debts with corresponding interest rates. Please, please include a line item for monthly savings. Saving for retirement, emergencies, and revolving savings (mentioned below) is crucial. It's best to have this taken out automatically, before you even realize it's gone. A healthy savings account is crucial for homeownership, and it's something to which you should always be adding. It's never too late to start. For expenses such as gas and utilities, it will be helpful to look through the previous year's statements and find an average (add each month's total and divide by 12) to enter into your monthly budget. It's always best with these estimates to make them conservative by padding a little extra money to your monthly amount if you're not exactly sure.

A lot of folks want to know if they should be working with their net or gross monthly income. Personally, I prefer net, and I just ignore anything taken out of your check automatically (such as 401(k), insurance, etc.), but please do whatever works best for you. There's really no wrong way to do it, just preferences.

Finally, I highly recommend including what's called revolving savings into your monthly budget. This isn't as fancy as it sounds. Basically, brainstorm any and all expenses that you expect to come up sporadically throughout the year, but that often sneak up on you. These kinds of expenses are what I call budget busters. You didn't plan for them on a monthly basis, so it's easy to throw the whole budget out with the bath water when you suddenly have to pay your car registration. Include things such as the aforementioned car registration, tuition, pest control, Mother's Day, birthdays, anniversaries, anything that you know will come up during the year. Make a conservative estimate for what they will all cost for the whole year, then divide that number by 12. You now have your monthly revolving savings set aside. If you forgot something as you're going along, no problem, just add it in, divide by 12 again, and there's your adjusted number. Note that if you have no savings currently, it will take some time to build up enough reserves to start covering these expenses, but go as slim as you need to for optional purchases, and eventually, this will be a great, stress-free system for you.

Whew, ok, budgeting is not so bad, right? Try my tips for at least a month, ideally longer, to get an idea of what is reasonable to expect, and what will work for you long-term. If you're at a point where you're feeling good about your finances, and any surprise expenses don't cause major mayhem, you're probably ready for what I call your post-house budget.

YOUR POST-HOUSE BUDGET

Hey, wait a minute, you don't even have a house yet. I know! But let's do a dry-run! By this time, you're a lean, mean, budgeting machine, so we're ready to venture into hypothetical territory. Go with me on this, because I promise, it's the best way to figure out how much house you can actually, *comfortably* afford.

Many of your expenses are going to be exactly the same, but several will change once you're in your home. It's time for another brainstorming session! Pull up a fresh budget sheet (or whatever you're using), and go through every line item to evaluate what will change once you're settled in your new home. The biggest will probably be your monthly housing payment, so let's just enter the number you came up with from the above section for now, but know that we're going to be playing around with this number. How much bigger is your new home, and how much extra will it cost to heat and cool it? If you're not sure, give your local utility office a call to get an estimate. Will you have to commute longer or shorter from your new location? Adjust your gasoline estimate accordingly. What else might change for you?

Keep going down your current budget and create your new, hypothetical budget. There will be some unknowns, but just do your best and be conservative where possible. Note that it will be wise to include a miscellaneous fund, as homes have a way of draining your wallet in unexpected ways. When I purchased my first home, I was surprised that with all the planning I had done, there were still thousands of dollars in expenses that I hadn't planned for specifically. Does your new home have a lawn? Well, buckle up, because that thing is going to cost way more than just a new lawn mower to maintain. Did the previous seller take all the curtains with them? You'll want to get some new blinds if you don't want the whole neighborhood to see you do your "new home dance." Ask any of your friends or family homeowners what expenses surprised them when they bought a home. Basically, count on the unexpected, and make sure you save enough money to be ready for it.

This can actually be fun, as you'll be doing a lot of visualization of yourself in your new home; but the most important part is figuring out if this new budget is going to work with your current income. Now that you have a better idea of how your current budget is going; could you handle this new payment along with all these other changes? Would it stretch you too thin? Play around with different numbers, see how far you could stretch an extra $100 if you bought a slightly less expensive home. Are you willing to make some other sacrifices to make it work? Are there ways you could cut back on your current expenses? Any way to bring in some extra income? These are all conversations you'll have to have with your spouse or any co-signers, because once you pull the trigger on your new home, it gets a lot less flexible.

Once you've thoroughly played around with your hypothetical "post-house budget," you should feel more confident in finding the monthly payment amount that you truly can afford. It doesn't matter if your lender says he'll loan you three times that; you know what you can afford better than anyone else. And once you have a monthly payment amount in mind and have entered it into one of the online calculators to find what price of house this would equate to, you'll be all set up to start your house search. There's this psychological phenomenon that happens when you see a house out of your price-range. All your budgeting and reasoning starts to weaken as you look for ways to own this beautiful house before you. If you only search and walk through what you can actually afford, we can skip this siren's song altogether. Ultimately, this is your choice, so plan thoroughly.

DOWN PAYMENTS AND SAVINGS

You know you want a house, but do you know how much will be required for a down payment? As usual, the answer is "it depends," but regardless of where you are in the process, it's generally a great idea to set aside as much as you can for both savings and a down payment. There will be those who advise you to only give the minimum required down payment; but I'm a big fan of paying as little interest as possible, so I'm always going to put down as much cash as I can, while still keeping a hearty amount in reserve for a rainy day.

The type of loan you select, which will be covered in step 6, will determine how much of a down payment will be required. In fact, for some loan types, you may not need to put any amount down. But generally speaking, you can expect approximately 3-5% of your loan amount to be required. In our $750 per month payment, $138,000 house example, this would be about $4,000 to $7,000. But again, just because you don't have to pay more, doesn't necessarily mean you should do that. Putting more money down would allow you to either take out a smaller loan, or purchase a more expensive home; and if you choose the former, you can expect to pay less interest over the life of the loan, and have a smaller monthly payment. Keep in mind that while I'm a fan of putting as much as possible toward a down payment, it shouldn't be at the expense of your savings. You'll want to keep a healthy reserve for the things we've discussed, not to mention any "usual" surprise expenses.

Another pro of paying a larger down payment is that if you can manage to come up with 20% of the home value, you won't have to pay monthly private mortgage insurance (we'll discuss PMI in step 6, but suffice it to say, it's basically you paying your lender's insurance that does you no good at all). But even if you can't quite scrounge that whopping 20%, paying extra will get you there sooner.

How much you pay for your down payment will need to be considered in balance with your savings. This can be a tricky thing to estimate, as there are one zillion things that could go wrong with a house, but may or may not happen. You'll have to weigh things carefully for yourself. How old is the house? Older homes tend to deteriorate faster. How old are the appliances? Could you cover a busted water heater? I just spent an exciting $1500 on mine, and let me tell you, it's a real blast. But in all seriousness, I'm so glad we had already set that aside for just such an occasion. I'll provide some resources at the end of this book to help give you a better idea of what kinds of expenses to expect as well as the general costs of homeownership. As a rule of thumb, it's best to save *at least $1,000 to $5,000* for emergencies, house or otherwise. And you know what I'm going to say by now: the more the better.

Are you feeling trepidatious? Understandable! But really, this all comes down to the old adage, "hope for the best, plan for the worst." You don't need to drive yourself crazy worrying about all the possible things that could go wrong with your new house, but it is wise to have money set aside, if nothing but for your peace of mind.

Let's say you're also getting a bit sad hearing these numbers. Maybe you just don't have that much saved up yet. No worries! Everyone has to start somewhere. And there is absolutely no shame in waiting. In fact, I have utmost respect for anyone wise enough to hold off on their wants in honor of sound financial choices. As I've mentioned, homeownership is not always the best choice; but that doesn't mean that will be the case forever. If you're already feeling stretched thin, take a deep breath, complete a budget, and set aside as much savings a month that you can. In fact, I would always recommend to clients that they "practice" with their hypothetical post-house payment estimate. Pretend that you're already in the house, but instead of paying that extra amount to your housing-related expenses, you set it aside in savings. Work hard to reduce expenses and/or increase income, and you'll have a hearty savings and down payment ready sooner than you may expect, I promise.

I will also mention briefly that down payments may be gifted from friends or family; however, I've seen that homeowners tend to do better making their monthly payments and expenses if they've worked hard, saved, and sacrificed for the entirety of their homes. But if you're lucky enough to have a rich and generous great uncle, more power to you!

DEBT

Can I ask you a personal question? You don't have to say it out loud. How much debt are you in? If you're not sure, you're definitely going to want to go pull all your statements and add them up. Even better, make a list of all your creditors, how much you owe them, what your minimum monthly payment is, and what interest rate you're paying [check out my free, simple worksheet for this in the resource section]. The reason you're going to want to have your total debt at hand is because this will be very important to your lender.

Lenders use a ratio called Debt-to-Income (DTI) to help them determine how much they should loan you. This is easy to calculate, as you just divide your total monthly debt and rent payments by your total gross income. Most lenders will require that this percentage be below 36 to 41%, possibly even higher or lower. For example, say you're grossing $3500 in income per month, and you have a rental payment of $800 (yes, rent is counted), a car payment of $300, a credit card payment of $75, and a student loan payment of $200. You would total up your debt payments ($800 + $300 + $75 + $200 = $1375), and divide that number by $3500 ($1375 / $3500 = .393). So in this example your DTI is .393, or 39.3%. In this example, yes, you may qualify for a loan, but this much debt would make me a little uneasy. Taking some time to pay off as much debt as you can before applying for a loan would be an excellent idea for several reasons, but you know your situation and your budget by now. The choice is, of course, yours.

CREDIT SCORES

Ah credit scores. A necessary evil in my opinion, shrouded in mystery. A mystery because while there's a lot we know about improving your score, the powers that be like to keep you guessing about specifics by withholding exactly how their algorithms work. And evil because in order to qualify for debt, you must have debt. Can I be honest for a second here? It's dumb. Credit scores are dumb. It's dumb that having more types of debt will improve your score, but if you've never been late on rent a day in your life? Nah, not important.

But now that I've got that off my chest, let's talk about why your dumb credit score is important. It plays a huge role in whether your lender will loan you money, how much she'll lend you, what interest rate she'll charge you, and will basically be the determining factor for whether or not you save potentially tens of thousands of dollars. There is a newer movement of lenders that don't rely on your credit score, and will instead accept utility and rent payments, but this is still a small faction, and I can't personally attest to their quality. I will, however, leave resources for you at the end of this book, if you have poor credit or no credit at all. Conventionally, though, you'll likely need to "play the game" and work to improve your score to get optimal loan terms.

So, what is your credit score? It's basically a number that's calculated based on your credit history, and is meant to provide lenders with an easy way to judge your creditworthiness. There are three credit bureaus, Experian, Equifax, and Trans Union, who collect and compile account information from your various creditors and accounts. And guess what? These guys can mess up. Big time. In fact, their data can have errors so large sometimes, it has been the difference between a loan approval and denial. The best way to handle this potential problem is to regularly check your credit reports, ideally well before you're applying for a loan and then have to deal with correcting an error during the homebuying process. Trust me, that's a headache you'll want to avoid.

You've probably heard all kinds of ads for a free credit report, but they are rarely actually free. The only place you need to go is www.annualcreditreport.com. This is the only site that's free of nonsense and will actually pull your report for free. That said, you only get one free report pull per year from each of the three credit bureaus, so this would end up being three free reports per year. Ideally, I like to space these out throughout the year so I can keep an eye on each bureau's accuracy and scan my report for any fraudulent behavior, but if you'll be applying for a loan soon, it's not a bad idea to pull all three at once to scan for any errors and problems. If you do find any issues on your report, each of the bureaus will have contact information for you to address the problem. Do this as soon as possible to avoid a headache down the road.

So you've checked your reports, they're free of errors, and you may be wondering, "well, where is this magical credit score? Those reports just had all my information and payment history, but no score." This can get confusing if you don't know the game, since everyone and their dog now offers their own score. Think of your credit report like raw ingredients. You'll need a recipe to calculate a score, but there are a bunch of recipes out there. The most popular recipe, and the only one that matters, is from a company called Fair, Isaac and Company, aka FICO. FICO has a proprietary algorithm, or math equation, that they apply to the raw data from your credit report. They then spit out your credit score, which ranges from 300 to 850, the higher the better. FICO scores are by far the most used by lenders, so this is the number you should care about. Other companies, even some of the credit bureaus themselves, offer their own algorithms (or recipes) to calculate their own scores, but if your lender doesn't use that score, it really isn't relevant.

It will no doubt surprise you that FICO will charge you money to see your actual score, so while your credit reports are free, pulling your score is not. There are some credit cards and premium plans offered that will give you access to your FICO score for free, but personally, I never bother pulling my FICO score. FICO has given broad hints about how their score is calculated (gotta keep that proprietary recipe at least partially shrouded in mystery), so I tell my clients to just focus on improving their score through the hints FICO has divulged, and then wait for your lender to actually pull your score. Note that pulling your own credit report and score will not ding your credit like a "hard pull" will, which is when you formally apply for credit.

So we know the whole credit score game is kind of a racket, yet it is, unfortunately, a crucial factor in getting your loan. The difference between an excellent score (over 720) and a decent one (650) can equate to tens of thousands of dollars for you, so it will be well worth your time to improve your score. Folks with good scores get prime interest rates and the most favorable loan terms, and a difference in even 1% on your interest rate could add potentially hundreds of dollars to your monthly payment, and tens of thousands to the total interest you pay over the life of the loan.

I'll list some resources for you, but to give you a very brief overview of best practices in regards to building and maintaining good credit, FICO has deigned to give us some hints. I'm not going to go too deeply into this, so please check out the resource section if you feel like you need additional help. The number one thing you should do, which accounts for the largest portion of your score, is to consistently make all your payments on time. If you have late payments in your past, the longer that time passes from those "negative events", the less impact they'll have on your score. If you have anything in collections, pay that off as soon as possible. Use less than about 30% of the credit available to you. Don't take out a bunch of new debt, especially in a short amount of time. Note that when it comes time to shop around for lenders, you'll have forty-five days to shop around as much as you'd like, and it will only count as one hard pull on your credit. Hard pulls ding your score slightly, so you'll want to avoid applying for too many sources of credit. If you have any old accounts that are in good standing, don't ever close those; they're helping your score. And lastly, this tip is from me, not FICO, but it is very good practice to regularly pull your reports and correct any mistakes, especially when you're planning to take out a large loan soon.

Lastly, on credit, to get approved for a loan, you'll need at least a score of around 620 for conventional loans, but you'll usually get best rates if it's over 720. The lender will pull a score using each of the three credit bureaus' data (yes, it can vary a bit between them; another good reason to check each bureau's report) for a total of three slightly different scores. He'll then use the middle score out of the three to determine what rates and terms you qualify for. Note that if you're applying for a loan with your spouse or a co-signer, the lender will pull the second person's three scores as well, take the middle score, and then pick the lower of the two co-signer's middle scores. All this to say, if someone is getting the loan with you, he/she will need to work to improve that score as well.

WHAT ELSE YOU SHOULD PREPARE

Of all the events in your life, the one that will require the most paperwork will probably be buying a house. No big deal, but you can definitely make the process run more smoothly if you find and compile documents beforehand. The basics that will likely be required are going to be two years of work history in W2 forms, tax documents, 30-60 days of pay stubs, two full bank statements, and personal documents such as social security cards and drivers licenses. If you can get these things scanned into a digital format, even better!

In terms of other things to do to make your process run more smoothly, it's a great idea to not make any large, undocumented deposits soon before you apply for a loan, and definitely not while you're waiting for loan approval. This can throw a big wrench in the underwriting process, so if you do have any big deposits to make, just be sure to speak with your lender first. Next, make sure that you don't incur any overdraft or penalty fees on any of your accounts. This again can derail a loan approval. And lastly, make sure that you indeed have the funds to close. Staging all of these things before you even apply for a loan will speed up the process and ensure far fewer possible delays and subsequent stress.

FIRST-TIME HOME BUYER'S PROGRAMS

The last thing to do before moving on to step three is to research if you qualify for any local first-time home buyer programs. Your city likely has access to funds that have been allocated for this. And trust me, don't assume you won't qualify without checking first. You'd be surprised how much money goes to various programs and who can qualify for them. Check out your local government, call the county clerk, ask your CPA, call your state's land grant university extension office and ask about free programs and grants. You will probably find something to help, especially if you are below the median income. There are a plethora of programs available, including sweat-equity, grants, tax credits, and free community workshops like the ones I participated in teaching; you just need to search your local institutions. If you're not sure where to start, enter your state into this website for more resources: https://www.nerdwallet.com/blog/mortgages/first-time-home-buyer-programs-by-state/

FINAL THOUGHTS

Hopefully, by now you have a good idea of how much of a home loan you can actually afford, as well as a place to start to get your financial foundation in order. Remember, if you take your time, start saving now, pay off as much debt as you can, start or continue to make all your payments on time, make and keep a budget—you will be setting yourself up for a lifetime of financial success inside or outside of a home. Follow the tips laid out in this chapter and you'll not only save yourself thousands of dollars, you'll also streamline your home buying process. If now is not the right time, don't be discouraged. If you stick to this plan, you'll be ready to move forward from a firm foundation, and you'll be so happy you did!

3

SHOP YOUR TEAM AND GET PRE-APPROVED: HOW TO SAVE THOUSANDS

Are you feeling great about your finances and know how much you can afford? You got some documents prepared and found an amazing first-time home buyer program in your city? Fantastic! Let's move on to the next step: shopping around for your real estate team and getting pre-approved.

LENDERS

I'm always surprised when I talk with family and friends to find out that they've made a big purchase without shopping around. Maybe it's because I'm extraordinarily cheap, but I don't spend $20 without looking for the best deal first. While you don't have to go crazy here, a home will likely be the biggest purchase you'll ever make, so it only makes sense that you would shop around for every aspect of that purchase that you can.

First up: your lender. You absolutely can and should shop around for your lender. So many folks just go with the first and only one they speak with, and this is a missed opportunity. There's more wiggle room in many of your loan fees than you may think, and most lenders are very eager for your business. This will likely make them willing to negotiate with you.

Here's what you'll do. Call up a lender. You might start with wherever you bank, a local credit union, a mortgage broker (more on the benefits of each in a bit). Tell them you're interested in a mortgage loan, as well as about how much money you'd like to borrow. (Remember, we already came up with this number, so it shouldn't really matter if you actually qualify for more.) Tell them you'll be shopping around, and to please give you their best estimates for loan costs. You'll provide them with the documents you already have on hand from the previous step. Get their estimate and pay attention to origination, application, and other fees, and especially the interest rate. Then call up another institution and repeat the same process. If the second guy's estimate of total closing costs is more than the first, tell him you've been speaking with someone else who can do better. If the second lender can't match or beat the first estimate, you'll be going with the first. Then do it all again with a third, and even fourth lender. Lenders often have various discounts and promotions, so really pit these guys against each other and make them work for your business—they *really* want it. Negotiate down to your best possible loan terms, and this will save you thousands of dollars both upfront and over the life of the loan.

Once you have your favorite lender with the most favorable loan terms, you can proceed to officially get pre-approved. Pre-approval is basically what it sounds like. You go through some preliminary screening and processing and get an unofficial go-ahead from your lender to start making offers on homes. While you don't have to do this before looking at homes, I would advise it in streamlining the process. If you've already been pre-approved, you'll be able to jump on hot deals and snag your dream house before someone else does. You'll be solidifying and formalizing all of the loan details once an offer is accepted. (We'll be covering all those loan details in step 6, but go on and peek ahead, if you would find that information helpful during the pre-approval phase.)

You should know that whenever you make an official inquiry for credit, this will count as a "hard pull" against your credit, which will pull your score down slightly. Luckily our credit overlords have allowed us that 45-day window to be able to shop around for mortgages, and have each of those hard pulls only count as one during that time frame. So don't let concern over your score stop you from shopping around!

I'll have some resources for you at the end of the book helping you find the best lender in your area, but let's briefly go over the main types you'll see: credit unions, local banks, mortgage banks, mortgage brokers, and even solely online entities.

Personally, I'm a big fan of credit unions for several reasons. You probably already bank with them, know them, trust them, and have access to their other banking services. If you ever need a home equity line of credit (HELOC), your credit union can provide that as well, so it's just easier logistically. Credit unions are also less likely to sell your loan to another company. (This isn't a huge deal, but it can be a minor hassle, so I'll touch on it briefly later in this book.) And best of all, you have access to a real person, face-to-face, to address any potential problems.

Now, some of these other lender options also offer similar benefits, so I won't say that any of the others are a bad idea at all, but this is just another testament to shopping around. Many people have asked me about mortgage brokers, and yes, an honest one can potentially save you time and fees; but in my experience, doing the footwork yourself by shopping around will ultimately land you with the most favorable results.

While you're negotiating with lenders, it's not a bad idea to start shopping around for the next member of your real estate team: your real estate agent. You could do this simultaneously, wait until after you've been pre-approved, or even before your pre-approval if you prefer. The order is up to you on this one!

REAL ESTATE AGENTS

Like any human, real estate agents come in many personalities. I've known several who are pushy, salesy and just rub me the wrong way, and even more who are helpful, hardworking, and motivated. Shopping for your agent probably won't be too hard, as you likely already know a dozen who have been bombarding you for years with their flyers and advertisements. You probably even have a cousin or a friend who has her license, but be careful not to be guilted or pressured into an agreement with family and friends. While this can definitely work out just fine, you'll want to pick the best agent for the job. You wouldn't want to unnecessarily limit the pool of hopefuls. But suffice it to say: real estate agents really, *really* want your business, too.

You may be asking, "but should I even use an agent? Don't lots of people just do it themselves? And yes, some people do. But believe me, I am the person who will do just about anything to save a buck, and I can tell you this is something you probably won't want to skimp on. Sure, there are people who are very familiar with the process, and yes, the internet has literally everything you could possibly want to know, but for first-time homebuyers, I highly recommend hiring a real estate agent. She will save you so much stress and time, it will be well worth it. And besides, as a buyer, you probably won't be paying anything out of pocket to use one, so you might as well. Let me explain.

Real estate agents are paid by commission, most often as a percentage of the sales price of the home. A common commission percentage is 6%, split between the buyer's agent and the seller's agent, so each earns 3% of the home's value. On a $300,000 home, for example, the seller's agent and the buyer's agent would make approximately $9,000 each. Holy cow, right? Another common practice is that these commissions come from the seller's home equity, so this is why I say you might as well use one as the buyer. Yes, one could argue that the agent commissions are already baked into the price of the home, so in a way, you may be technically paying for it, but regardless, it will be worth it to hire one. The commission fee is, in theory, negotiable, but this matters much more when you're ready to sell your home.

Let's talk about some of the things your agent will do for you to earn that hefty commission. First of all, they represent you and your best interests. If you go to buy a home that is listed with a seller's agent, that agent has the seller's best interest at heart, not yours. Having a real estate agent gives you access to a professional advocate during the entire process. Your buyer's agent will assist you at all phases of this process, start to finish. Any question that comes up for you at any point, your best bet is to ask your agent. From finding and touring homes, to making an official offer and handling the copious paperwork, a good agent will have you covered. She will act as a liaison between you and the seller, speak up for you at closing, and make sure the process runs as smoothly as possible on a structured timeline. She likely already has a wide network of fellow real estate professionals and can recommend home inspectors, lenders, and anyone else you might need along the way. She can also help you negotiate the very best price for your home, shaving potentially thousands off the asking price.

I loved my first real estate agent. Months after our closing, after she'd already walked into the sunset with her well-earned paycheck, we had some issues with our county's tax department and were going to be charged more than we should have been. Not knowing who to talk to, I called our agent and she said, "Nope. They can't do that. I'll call you right back." And indeed, a few minutes later, she called to tell me that she had taken care of the problem and we wouldn't be charged the additional amount. She was a bulldog for us and I still love her for all the help she gave us.

The takeaway here is that a buyer's agent is definitely worth it; in fact, you will be disadvantaged without one. So take your time on this search as well. Shop around for the very best agent; not just one who has many contacts and has sold many houses (although that's important, too), but one whom you like on a personal level. You'll be spending some time walking through houses together, so it would be quite the bummer if you can't stand her. Between your lender and your agent, if you do this right and shop around for the best fit, you will be saving yourself a good deal of money and time.

A QUICK WORD ABOUT REAL ESTATE ATTORNEYS

Some people say that a real estate attorney is a necessary addition to your real estate team. Personally, I haven't seen a good case for that, assuming you're not dealing with a wildly unique property with liens and easements and squatters inside. For the vast majority of people, I believe a real estate agent is enough. However, there are some state laws and some rare situations where an attorney would be required. If you suspect you may require additional legal assistance, I'll provide some resources for you at the end of this book; but for most of you, go ahead and take a pass on the real estate attorney.

All right, you've got a great lender, a fantastic real estate agent, and you're pre-approved: let's get ready for my favorite part!

4

FIND THE PERFECT HOME AND ENJOY NO REGRETS

D earest reader, you should know something about me: I have a tendency to get a tad obsessed with subjects that interest me, perhaps even to an unhealthy degree. And would you like to know what one of my top interests is? I bet you can guess, but I'll give you a second. You ready? That's right. It's houses. Give me all the floor plans, home decor, and exterior designs. I check Zillow.com daily for homes in my area. I get so excited about a new floor plan release from my favorite builder, my family asks me to chill out. I taught myself how to use drafting software so I could design my own house plans. I've painted mockups for my dream home's exterior. It may be safe to posit that I am obsessed with homes. But all of this is to say that you've come to the right place, if you're hoping to discover how to find your perfect home.

So right off the bat, you should know that there are many different types of houses. You've got your single-family units (what you probably think of when you think of a house), multi-family units, town houses, condos, manufactured homes, and new construction. (There are even more options than this, but these are the most common you'll see.) Before we talk about what might be the best fit for you, let's talk about some pros and cons to each.

SINGLE-FAMILY UNITS

Ah, the American dream, barbecuing out in your fenced backyard. Your walls won't be attached to any neighbors' units, so you can enjoy more privacy, have more space, and listen to movies as loudly as you'd like. These types of homes are often larger than other options, have larger yards, and unless you're part of a Homeowner's Association (HOA), you can essentially do anything you'd like to the home, inside or out. The downside of these is that with all that freedom, you're largely left on your own to deal with any damages and repairs. If you'd prefer living inside city limits rather than suburban or rural areas, single units can also be harder to find. In addition to this, you might not want to take care of a yard; and if you've never taken care of one before, believe me, it's more work and time than you think it will be. Lastly, membership in an HOA can be compulsory when you purchase certain homes; and while HOAs can offer many benefits, I'm personally not a fan at all. If I want to paint my front door turquoise, I think I should be able to, thank you very much.

MULTI-FAMILY UNITS

When you hear multi-family units, most likely you'll be thinking of a duplex, but there are many properties that offer three or more units in one building. One of the biggest advantages for these is a technique called "house hacking." I really wish I would have done this when I was first married. House hacking is when you purchase a duplex, live in one of the units, and rent out the other. The rent from the other unit goes toward or fully covers your mortgage payment. It's a sweet setup. Many people enjoy multi-family units if they live with large, extended families who want to live together, but not necessarily in the same house. A con of multi-family units is the shared wall and close proximity to neighbors. That's not a big deal for everyone, though. Multi-family units can also be a bit tricky to finance, and typically don't appreciate in value as much as single-family units.

TOWN HOUSES

Town houses can be a great, cheaper option for new homeowners looking to start building equity. You will share one or two walls with neighbors attached at either side, but if you don't belt out Broadway songs throughout the day, this likely won't be a problem for you. Town homes are usually built in premium areas where housing can be scarce, so if proximity to downtown or beautiful scenery is important to you, this can be a great option. The yards are usually extremely small, which could be a pro or a con for you, and they can operate with or without an HOA, which again could be a pro or a con for you. It would be rare, though, to find a townhome that does not have at least minimal HOA fees. The biggest con of a townhouse is when it comes time to sell. This will vary by location, but think about it. You and three of your neighbors may be selling the exact same unit at the same time. With supply and demand, you may find yourself being undercut and need to sell for less than you had hoped.

CONDOS

A condo, or condominium, is basically a unit that you own, inside a big building that you don't own. There are usually common areas (also not owned by you), and certain rules you'll need to follow. The main pro of these units are the amenities. You may have access to pools, gyms, parks, lawn, massages, and more, none of which you are responsible to maintain. Of course, you will be paying for these things through fees. Condos also *can* be less expensive than an equivalent single-family unit of similar square footage. They are usually located in prime downtown areas as well, which you may value. The main cons are the potentially high costs for all those amenities. You're also crammed in with a lot of other people, some of whom you may wish were not at such proximity. Although, neighbors can be problematic anywhere you go, and whatever house type you select.

MANUFACTURED

I know what you may be thinking, but these are actually way nicer these days than you may think. Not to be confused with mobile homes and trailers, manufactured homes are basically pre-fabricated at a factory, shipped to your location and assembled by professionals. That doesn't necessarily sound bougie, but go to YouTube and check out some of the beautiful, spacious manufactured homes that are available. These homes are usually far less expensive than any other option, and most offer almost any modern feature you may be looking for. The biggest con for manufactured homes is that they tend to offer very little appreciation; many even depreciate over time. It can sometimes be challenging to work with zoning codes to find a lot where they will be allowed. There can also be a stigma associated with manufactured homes, but my guess is that this may vanish over time, as nicer and roomier models continue to be sold.

NEW CONSTRUCTION

As you may expect, new construction comes with many pros and cons as well, the biggest advantage being that you can get almost exactly what you want in a home. If you're like me, you've considered that you don't want guests to be able to see inside your bedroom from the front door, that you don't care about a third car garage, and that you require copious amounts of natural sunlight. If your wishlist includes dozens of these kinds of preferences, building a home may work best for you. You'll get to pick your floor plan, your lot, your fixtures and paint colors, how much you spend, and more; although this can be overwhelming to people who don't draw pictures of these things in their spare time. It's also a brand spanking new home, and doesn't the idea that no one else's skin cells are settled in its crevices help you sleep at night? Just me?

And of course, the biggest downside is the time and potential stress of such a large undertaking. Not all builders are created equal, and I'm sure you know someone who will talk for hours about the nightmare they had building. You also may find that the "endless options" you had hoped for are more limited than you think, depending on your builder. Construction can take anywhere from 4 to 8 months, or way more, depending on your area, your builder, and your plans.

There are many more pros and cons to new construction, as well as the previous home-types I've listed, so I'll provide more resources for you at the end of this book if you're interested in learning more. As you can see, your particular situation and the type of home it may call for can vary widely. Take some time to think about what will work best for you and your family.

SOME THINGS TO CONSIDER WHEN CHOOSING YOUR HOME

Here are several questions to ask yourself before and during your house search. Hopefully, they will get you thinking in new ways.

Most importantly, what is the top price of home you can actually afford in your budget? I would highly recommend that when you start searching online, you filter out all homes above that price, and tell your real estate agent to do the same. Bigger, nicer houses really are like the siren's song; you'll be rethinking your entire budget, if you accidentally fall in love.

What are your family's needs and wants? Will those change anytime soon? For older folks, you may want to consider a house with fewer stairs.

What kind of location are you looking for? If you have or plan to have children, how are the local schools? How far is the commute to work?

If you do have those kids, will you have enough bedrooms for them? How about if you decide to have more kids?

How long do you plan to stay there? Generally speaking, if you plan to stick around for fewer than 4-7 years, it may not be worth the exorbitant closing costs associated with the home purchase. If your time frame is shorter, renting may actually be more advantageous to you.

What do you expect regarding the resale of the home? Would it be worth it to build that third car garage, since most homes in the area have one and future buyers will expect it?

Do you want to take care of a big yard? If not, do you have the funds to hire help?

How important is privacy to you? Do you want to be able to play your electric guitar at full volume without getting yelled at by a neighbor?

These are just some ideas to get the ball rolling; but really take your time with this. It will be worth the effort to take everything about your situation into consideration.

RESOURCES FOR FINDING YOUR HOME

Your best resource on this one will be your real estate agent. After you've given some thought to the above questions, and any other considerations for your unique circumstances, tell your agent exactly what you're looking for. What are your must-haves and what are your nice-to-haves? Can you list them by priority? Be as clear as possible, and your agent will start scouring the markets to find a match for you.

While your agent searches, there are an increasing number of databases that are accessible to homebuyers as well. One of my favorites is www.zillow.com. It's a free site that will let you filter your search by just about any metric, such as number of bedrooms, bathroom, square footage, year built, and much more. If you scroll down on any home listing, Zillow also has a handy online calculator so you can quickly get an estimate of how much your payment would be for that very house. You'll just enter how much money you have to put down and the interest rate you expect to have on the loan, and you'll get a pretty decent idea of the total monthly cost. Just keep in mind that it won't be exact, as there will be many more factors that go into your actual payment.

You can also search many statewide or local websites that will have a lot of overlap, but sometimes several homes that weren't listed elsewhere. Find these through Google or by asking your agent. You can also check your local classifieds page, both in online papers and through social media. I have come across several gems that were only listed through a Facebook group and nowhere else, so keep your eyes peeled!

When you find a promising home, ask your agent to set up an appointment to walk through it. This is a very important step, as you really can't get the feel of a home until you see it in person.

Photographs have the tendency to misrepresent the actual space. I've walked through homes that looked so great in the photos, but when we got there, we saw that the layout was actually really awkward and with far too little natural light for my tastes. Likewise, some homes had poor quality photos that didn't do the home justice. This is honestly my very favorite part of the process, but if you're not a giant nerd like me, and this isn't what you would prefer to do with your time, trust me that you'll want to do it anyway. The more homes you walk through, the more you'll be able to dial in on exactly what you like and ultimately choose.

A WORD ON STYLE

As you begin your home search, you'll start to get a better feel for your style, your likes and dislikes; themes will start to emerge for you regarding trends and local quirks. For instance, in my county, for some reason, the vast majority of the homes are ramblers, with a very similar layout, and a garage that protrudes so far in front of the house, it's like the house was an afterthought. There's nothing inherently wrong with these thousands and thousands of houses, but where I prefer a classic, two-story home with colonial vibes, it has been very difficult for me to find my dream house. In your own search, you may want to consider these things. And remember, even if the home's aesthetics aren't important to you, they likely will be to someone else when you eventually sell it.

Do you like the charm of older homes, or do you like to be assured in a new home that no one has ever been murdered there? Apparently ghosts can be a real nuisance. But seriously, there's a lot to consider with older homes. You're more likely to get a beautiful, mature yard, in an established neighborhood, but you'll also be more likely to be doing repairs. So how handy are you? Would you be willing to do some renovations on a home that needs it for a more discounted sales price?

Some other considerations: Do you like a more modern, open layout? Resale can be hard with some of these older homes that are chopped into smaller living spaces. Do you care about good landscaping? It can cost tens of thousands of dollars to put a new one in, or fix the current one. Do all your neighbors have a pool? If yours is the only one in the neighborhood that doesn't, this can affect your home value negatively. Do you care about being in an HOA? This can limit some of your freedoms, but also provide certain benefits, such as snow removal and yard maintenance. Always remember to factor in any HOA fees to your total monthly payment.

Do you want a home that's following the current trends, or something more timeless, like brick with white trim? I love some of these current home trends I've been seeing, but it's a good idea to keep a long-term viewpoint. Remember, at one point, everyone thought that shag carpet and faux wood paneling was a good idea.

Are you going to want a shop in your garage? Will you need a third car garage? Do you prefer a rambler or a two-story? Will stairs be a problem now or in the future? The more you search for and walk through houses, the better sense you'll get for popular trends in your area, and what you'll find useful or necessary in your own home.

HONING IN ON YOUR WINNER

While I do suggest looking at several homes, there is such a thing as decision paralysis. Some people will have that lightbulb moment and just know which house is "the one." But this just isn't the case for everyone. For you, it might be a matter of making a pros and cons list, weighing your options carefully, and pulling the trigger. I hate to admit this, even to myself, but there really is no perfect house. Even if you build your "dream house," there will still be mistakes and elements you wish you had done differently.

In the end, you'll want to give yourself plenty of time in your search. Walk through a reasonable number of homes, and if one feels right, fits in your budget, and meets at least your needs list and a few items from your wants list, don't think *too* hard about it. For my first home, it fit this criteria, but I was still nervous to make an offer. Nerves will probably be present for your first home offer, but once you finish this book, you'll overwhelm those nerves with the confidence that comes from knowledge. You got this!

5

MAKE AN OFFER THAT WILL LET YOU SLEEP AT NIGHT

Y ou've found your home—how exciting! But before you get carried away planning the living room layout, we need to make sure no one else snags it out from under you. It's time to make an offer!

Depending on when and where you're reading this, you might find yourself in a buyer's market or a seller's market. It's basic supply and demand: if there are more buyers than sellers in your area, seller's will have the upper hand in a seller's market. However, if there are more homes available than there are buyers, you're in a buyer's market and you will likely have an upper hand in negotiations. You can absolutely purchase a home in either market, but there will be certain considerations based on the market you find yourself in. At the time of writing this, it has been a seller's market in the majority of U.S. locales for many years now, so it's very likely you're looking for a home in a seller's market. I should also note that many analysts suspect it will continue to be this way for years to come, so there's likely no need to hold out for a buyer's market in most cases. Homes will likely continue to appreciate each and every year.

In a seller's market, you as a home buyer will have less leverage in negotiating a deal for the home. You'll likely be in competition with other buyers, so you'll need to act swiftly and be willing to make a more attractive offer for the home you want. Back when I purchased my home, it was more of a buyer's market, so we offered an amount under the asking price, proposed that the seller pay for all the closing costs, and made several other contingencies to our offer. In a seller's market, this would be fairly ridiculous. In that same neighborhood today, a house that is put up for sale will likely have several offers within a couple of days, usually over the asking price. Your real estate agent should be very familiar with the temperature of your local market, so rely on her to know how sweet you need to make your offer.

You may have walked through the home, fell in love, and are ready to make an offer right now, but hold up. There are several considerations before you make your offer official. The most obvious one is: does it fit within your budget? Hopefully you haven't even been touring homes outside your budget, but if you are in a hot seller's market, you may need to be prepared to offer an amount over the listing price. Be sure to account for this possibility.

Another consideration is whether or not any repairs will need to be done to the home. You'll have your chance later in the process to have a professional come and inspect everything, and appropriate adjustments can be made then, but you should be able to have a pretty good sense whether there are any glaring repairs that need to be made. Plus, the homeowner should have made a list of needed repairs he knows about that your agent should provide to you. If you were hoping for a move-in-ready home, pay close attention to this. For older homes, it's very likely there will be at least some work that needs to be done.

You should also consider whether the price the seller is asking is fair. It seems like sellers can ask for increasingly ridiculous amounts, but you'll still want to be sure that you're getting a fair deal. Your agent can perform a comparative market analysis (CMA) on the home in question, which basically compares similar homes that have sold recently nearby, and will be able to tell you whether or not the asking price is in line or not.

When crafting an offer, you'll also need to consider any contingencies. These are essentially clauses that will allow you to walk away from the contract if certain conditions are not met. Most commonly, these will include an appraisal, an inspection, a clean title, and that you're able to secure financing. So if an inspection shows that the home needs a $12,000 new roof, you can then alter your agreement to reduce your offered price, ask the seller to replace it, keep the offer as it stands, or withdraw it entirely if you can't come to an agreement.

Contingencies are a very important part of your offer, so speak with your agent and thoroughly go over anything you may wish to add. When I made my offer, I asked that the seller clear out all the dead bugs from the garage, but keep in mind, this was in a buyer's market. You'll probably need to clean out your own dead bugs in a hot seller's market.

EARNEST MONEY

Next up, you'll need to discuss with your agent how much earnest money to offer. Earnest money is basically an amount you're willing to pay to show that you are serious about the offer. It will be held in a third party escrow account, and you will lose it all if you breach your end of the agreement. Because a seller will take his house off the market while the deal is being processed, if you end up backing out, the seller will have to start again from scratch. Relisting his home and dealing with all that wasted time can be a big financial hit, so he gets to keep your earnest money as compensation.

If, however, the deal falls through due to a problematic inspection, or any other contingencies you made in your offer, you get to walk away with your earnest money. Assuming the deal goes through as planned, that earnest money will go toward either your down payment or closing costs. Earnest payments are typically 1-3% of the home price, but depending on your area and how hot the market is, your agent will have the best advice for you as to how much exactly will be attractive to the seller. You don't need to be concerned about losing it if you are genuinely interested in purchasing the home, intend to actually buy it, and include all the necessary contingencies in your offer.

Ultimately, when crafting your offer, you'll want to try and get as many seller concessions as you can, while still making your offer attractive and reasonable. Much of this will depend on your local market, so I would advise you to listen to your real estate agent's input. She knows your specific market better than you or I do. If you can get the seller to pay closing costs, fantastic. If not, it may still be worth it to you to get the home you love.

MAKING YOUR OFFER

Once you have discussed all of the above considerations with your agent, it's time to officially make your offer. Here's where you'll be glad that you hired a real estate agent. She's going to take care of all of this for you. Yes, you'll need to discuss everything with her, and you will definitely want to read everything you sign, but your agent will draft up all the boring forms, fill in the information correctly, and advise you on the most advantageous variables. I remember that my agent had brought along a physical copy of a purchase agreement to our walk-through and all we had to do was skim through it, initial and sign it. She took care of the rest and kept us posted on all the communications with the seller's agent.

What will happen next is likely some back-and-forth between your agent and the seller's agent. The seller may immediately accept your first offer, or he may submit a counteroffer. You'll then need to decide whether or not to accept this offer. You'll go back and forth like this until an agreement is accepted by both parties.

Included in your offer will be an estimated closing date, which may change during that time frame. It's set for a date in the future, usually 5-6 weeks out, to give everyone involved in the processing enough time to finish their tasks. (These will be discussed in detail in subsequent steps.)

A quick note on closing costs, which will be covered in detail in step 8, since it has some relevance to your offer. Closing costs can be expensive, typically 2-5% of the home's value. Assuming you can't get the seller to cover some of the cost, this could potentially blow your budget. There is an option I'm reluctant to tell you about, because I don't think it's a good idea. But if this is make or break for you, you should know that most lenders are willing to give you a credit toward closing costs if you agree to accept a higher interest rate on your loan. Generally speaking, this isn't a great idea. The interest rate can be deceiving in how small it looks. But over fifteen or thirty years, a small difference in interest rate can add up to tens of thousands of dollars. So consider this cautiously. In my opinion, it's far better to build up more savings to be able to cover closing costs. You can also usually wrap up some or all closing costs into your actual loan; but again, the less debt the better, in my humble opinion.

Ok. Your offer has been accepted. Congratulations! This is so exciting! You're ready to move onto the next step: applying for your mortgage. Your agent will be taking care of a lot of things behind the scenes, and multiple tasks will likely be happening at once. But I'll be focusing on your job and what you need to know. So let's go!

6

APPLY FOR YOUR MORTGAGE: FAST-TRACK THE PROCESS AND AVOID COSTLY MISTAKES

Hooray! Your offer has been accepted! Hopefully, if you've followed all of my tips so far, you'll already be saving yourself thousands of dollars. And from the last step, you've negotiated with the seller for fair terms, and avoided losing your earnest money. So let's get down to business and officially apply for your mortgage.

If you followed step two, you've already been pre-approved by your favorite lender. This is going to save you a lot of time and effort in this step. And now that you're officially applying for your financing, the faster you give your lender any documents she asks for, the faster this part will go. If you're in a particular rush to speed this along, feel free to ask your lender about something called a "full-submit." You would ask about this when you first selected her as your lender during pre-approval. This is basically "pre-underwriting" to get the ball rolling sooner on official approval while you're searching for a home and making offers. Not all lenders will allow this, but there's no harm in asking if you're eager to move in sooner.

Recall from step two that your credit score is going to matter a great deal when locking in your official interest rate. Anything over 720 will likely get you the best, prime rates, and anything below 620 will likely get you a denial for financing (unless you select a certain loan type I'll discuss in just a moment). You, and your spouse, if you have one, will want to take this into consideration well before you apply for your loan. You're not going to want to add "haggling with the credit bureaus" to your to-do list while you're trying to buy a home. Recall that both borrowers' scores will be pulled, and the lower of the two middle scores is the one the lender will use. If your spouse's credit is significantly worse than yours, you may consider putting the loan in your name only; but be aware that this can cause potential problems, aside from relational ones. You wouldn't be able to count your spouse's income, and thus might not qualify for as big of a loan. Plus, the underwriter of the loan may still consider your spouse's debt in your debt-to-income ratio (DTI). Basically, it can get a little sticky, but it is certainly an option.

WHAT LOAN TYPE IS BEST FOR YOU?

You've already checked out your credit score, you know how much money you have to use as a down payment, and you've already calculated your DTI. (Recall that this is just adding up your total monthly debt, including your rent payment, and dividing that by your gross monthly income. Expressed as a percentage, you'll want to keep this below 41-45% to qualify for a loan, or possibly even lower than that for some lenders.) Knowing these factors will help you decide what loan type is best for you.

There are four main types of loans: FHA, VA, USDA, and Conventional. Each one comes with different requirements and considerations, so I'll go over each one and help you decide which one makes the most sense given your credit score, down payment, DTI, and other qualifications.

FHA Loans:

First up is an FHA loan. These loans are insured by the government through the Federal Housing Administration (FHA). They are popular among many first-time home buyers, as they allow more leniency in their qualifications. With a mere 3.5% of the home's value required as down payment, FHA loans are an attractive option for those who are struggling to save up the necessary funds. I will caution you though, as your overly cautious friend, that just because something is offered to you that requires less from you, that doesn't necessarily mean you should take it. As I've said, I'm a big fan of taking on as little debt as possible.

The other big draw of these loans is the less stringent credit score requirement. You may be able to have a score as low as 580, which would be unacceptable to conventional lenders. You also have the option of paying a higher percentage as down payment in exchange for an even lower acceptable credit score, even as low as 500. If you have recent bankruptcies or foreclosures on your report, you may still qualify for an FHA loan. Now, if you have a 500 credit score, I would highly advise you to first work on repairing it, incorporating healthier financial habits to ensure your chances of long-term success as a homeowner. If you're not ready to own a home yet, I just don't want to see you set up for the intense stress and heartache it can bring to those who weren't adequately prepared. You'll be ready someday, just follow step two and take your time!

I know not everyone will listen to me on that, but let's continue discussing FHA loans, as they can still be a good option for those who are actually fully prepared to buy a home. FHA loans will allow you to have a 43% DTI, and possibly even higher, although you would have to meet certain conditions, and likely need to compensate with a higher credit score. You can also use FHA loans to purchase any of the home types I mentioned in step four (condos, single-family units, multi-family units, townhouses, and even manufactured homes). There are no income limits to this type of loan.

You may be thinking, "hot diggity, sign me up!" But not so fast. There are some big downsides to FHA loans as well, the biggest being mortgage insurance. Mortgage insurance is basically how lenders protect themselves from you possibly defaulting on your payments, i.e., failing to pay on time and possibly going into foreclosure. You will pay some form of this insurance premium on most types of loans, but there are some key differences in the length of time you'll be paying, and how much the payment is. For conventional loans, if you have less than 20% for your down payment, you will be charged private mortgage insurance premiums until your home equity reaches 20%. (More on this in the conventional loan section.) With FHA loans, you will be paying your insurance premium for the entire duration of the loan. This is a huge bummer since this payment doesn't help you in any way; it only protects the lender. For FHA loans, this premium is referred as MIP (mortgage insurance premium), and you'll additionally be required to pay an upfront premium of 1.75% of the loan, regardless of down payment. MIP rates range from 0.45% to 1.05% of the loan, and depends on your loan-to-value ratio and mortgage term. This can easily add an extra hundred dollars to your payment, or even more, so it's certainly worth considering.

FHA loans also have more restrictive housing standards and you may encounter some hiccups with older properties. Each county has set loan limitations as well, which can be problematic in more expensive areas. If you're planning to rent out your home or buy a vacation property, an FHA loan won't work for you, as the funds must go toward your primary residence. These loans can also take longer to process, which equates to all kinds of potential issues. All in all, if you can qualify for a conventional loan, I would recommend that route over FHA loans. They are certainly there for certain situations, but if given the choice, a conventional loan will most often be more favorable.

To summarize, this type of loan may suit you if you have less money to put down, a lower credit score, and a higher DTI. However, your options will be more restrictive and you'll pay higher insurance costs over the life of the loan. Keep in mind, you could refinance into a different loan type at any point, but this will incur more closing costs and hassle.

VA Loans

This type of loan is only going to apply to service members, veterans, and eligible surviving spouses, so I'll just hit the main points, as the Department of Veteran's Affairs will be able to give you a much more detailed rundown (check out the resource section). Basically, if you qualify for a VA loan, I typically recommend that you choose this option. It can be a hassle to work with the VA on anything, but this loan will offer you a fantastic interest rate and flexible payments. VA loans are one of the only types that does not require mortgage insurance; plus closing costs are usually capped, which is a big flipping deal. You will still have to pay a funding fee as a percentage of the loan amount, but this can be rolled into the loan. VA loans also don't require a down payment. But please remember, just because you can, doesn't mean you should. This is still a loan that you will need to pay back with interest. Consider putting some hearty amount down, even though VA loans don't require it. My brother served in Afghanistan with the army, and he and his wife enjoy mortgage terms I wish I had. You veterans earned this privilege though, so take advantage of it if you can!

USDA Loans

When you think of the United States Department of Agriculture (USDA), do you think about mortgages? I sure don't. And yet, this is indeed another type of loan you may be interested in if you're building in a rural area. What, exactly, is a rural area? Well, you'll have to check the USDA's website, as they have set their own location qualifications. You might be surprised, though, what counts as rural. I'm five minutes away from a city that qualifies, and I'm within a ten minute drive to two different Walmarts.

Assuming you're looking to buy a home in an official rural area, you'll also need to meet certain income restrictions in order to qualify for a USDA loan. This amount will be determined by each county. You'll also need to plan on occupying the home as your primary residence. The main advantage of these loans is that they also do not require a down payment. (My same advice applies here, as it does to FHA and VA loans.) There are actually several subtypes of USDA loans, most of which will also require mortgage insurance, will often offer low interest rates, and will work with people who have lower credit scores. The USDA has many grants and programs for eligible home buyers and owners, so it's worth checking it out on their site (see my resource section) or talking to your lender about it.

Conventional Loans

If you're like me, picking the "conventional option" doesn't usually sound very fun. But in this case, I will tell you that conventional loans will often offer you the most favorable terms, assuming you can qualify. Yes, they require higher down payments and credit scores, and yes, a lower DTI will likely be necessary, but they make up for it with several advantages. The main one being that overall borrowing costs tend to be lower, even if your interest rate is a tad higher. The loans can be used for any type of home, and it doesn't have to be your primary residence. Some lenders will let you pay as little as 3% for your down payment, which is very competitive with the other loan types. And my personal favorite advantage is that you're not stuck with mortgage insurance for the life of the loan.

Let's get into mortgage insurance for a second before I talk about some disadvantages to this type of loan. Where mortgage insurance for FHA loans is called mortgage insurance premium, or MIP, you'll hear it called private mortgage insurance, or PMI, when applied to conventional loans. As I mentioned, if you are providing less than 20% of home's value as down payment, you'll be saddled with PMI as part of your monthly payment (unless there's some rare lender promo going on). These rates usually range from .58% to 1.86%, depending on your credit score, loan-to-value ratio, and DTI, so it would be reasonable to expect to pay hundreds of dollars per month for this. That being the case, we're going to want to get rid of that portion of your as soon as possible.

I mentioned that PMI can be removed on conventional loans, and if you're paying hundreds per month for it, it makes sense to eliminate it as soon as you can. Coming up with a 20% down payment may not be feasible for everyone, so the next best thing is to make extra payments on your loan. I'll get into this more at the end of this chapter, but essentially, the sooner you build up your home equity to pass that 20% mark, the sooner you start pocketing those premiums.

Here's a nifty trick as your equity starts nearing that 20% mark. By law, your mortgage servicer needs to automatically remove your PMI payment once your equity has surpassed 22% of the original home's value. But you're allowed to request it sooner than that, once you pass the 20% threshold. For example, let's say your home appraised at, and sold for, $200,000 when you purchased it, and you originally paid $20,000 (or 10%) as a down payment. Your loan would be for $180,000 (that's the $200,000 home price minus your $20,000 down payment). At that point, you had 10% equity in your home. You've been making extra payments, and now your loan has been reduced to $160,000. Assuming the home is still worth $200,000 (it's likely gone up in value, but let's keep this example simple), you now have 20% equity (that's your $200,000 home value, minus your loan of $160,000 equals

$40,000; and $40,000 divided by your home value of $200,000 equals 20%).

The math here isn't as important as the concept. The point is that you're allowed to contact your mortgage servicer and request PMI be removed well before they are legally required to do it on their own. That extra 2% of equity (the legally required 22% versus the 20% you now have) is a full $4,000 in additional equity in our example. That's a whole lot of time to be waiting around, paying a needless PMI premium while you wait for your servicer to get around to removing it automatically! You'll need to make your request in writing and meet a few other requirements, but I'll provide a resource for this at the end of the book for you to check out.

All right, now that we have a good understanding of PMI, let's get back to some of the disadvantages of conventional loans. I've already mentioned most of them—qualification for these loans can be difficult. You'll need your credit score above 620, you'll usually need a lower debt-to-income (DTI) ratio, and though private mortgage insurance (PMI) does eventually get removed, it will still add a cost to your payment for a while. These types of loans also require a great deal of paperwork and verification of various elements such as income, employment, debt, assets, and more. The takeaway is that if you have a good credit score, a lower debt load, a stable income history, and a down payment of at least 3%, a conventional loan will probably be your best bet (except for you veterans).

Other Loan Types

You may have heard of other loan types such as interest-only loans, jumbo loans, adjustable rate mortgages, and others. For the most part, these either will not apply to you, or won't be helpful to you. After the housing crash back in 2009, the government has required lenders to be much more transparent about their terms. But in the rare case you see something like a balloon payment or prepayment penalty, do not accept it.

LOAN TERMS

Oh boy, does that subtitle get you excited, or what? Actually, if you want to start an argument between two financial experts, ask them whether you should take out a 15-year or 30-year loan. I'm in the mood to argue, so let's do this.

In all honesty, there are pros and cons to each route, and as usual, it is ultimately up to you to weigh your options. The main advantage of a 15-year loan is that you will usually get a better interest rate, and thus pay far less money in total interest payments over the life of the loan. You'll also be loan-free in 15 years, which is a pretty sweet deal. These advantages, however, come with a much larger monthly payment, which might limit the size loan you'll be able to take. A 30-year loan will have lower monthly payments, but with the extra time and slightly higher interest rate, you'll end up paying much more interest over the life of the loan. Some argue that you'll get to deduct all that interest from your taxes, and while that's true, I'm just not very impressed with the concept that you save money by spending more.

Let's break down a quick example, and then I'll tell you which option I prefer. Say you take out a loan for $200,000, putting $10,000 down (that's a 5% down payment). And let's say the interest rate on a 15-year mortgage is 2.7%, where the 30-year loan offers 3.2%. In this scenario, your 15-year monthly payment would be $1,285, with a total loan cost (down payment, principal, and interest) of $241,277. The 30-year payment would only be $822 per month, but your total loan cost would be a whopping $305,808. (I'll provide a link to an online calculator in the resource section so you can play around with these numbers for yourself. Your lender will also be able to provide you with a side-by-side comparison.) Note that the 15-year payment isn't twice as big as the 30-year. This is largely because of the difference in interest rate, but that big of a difference in monthly cost could be the difference between a sustainable home payment and an unsustainable one.

So what should you do? You'll notice that the tiny difference in interest rates, combined with double the loan repayment time, saves you almost $65,000 in interest payments to go the 15-year route. Holy cats, that's a ton of money! That being the case, you might think you know which option I'm going to advise you to pick. But actually, this is where half the experts might argue with me. My preference is actually to pick a 30-year mortgage, but make payments *pretending* like you have a 15-year loan. Why would you do this? Well, I'm a huge fan of financial security, and I like to plan for the worst. Let's see an example.

Take the numbers from my previous example. Let's say you picked the 30-year loan and your minimum payment is $822 per month. You've been very careful with your budgeting and can actually afford to pay $1250 per month, it would just feel a little tight. Though you're only required to send in $822 per month, you actually send in $1250 per month, and designate that the extra $428 ($1250 minus $822 equals $428) go toward paying down your principal balance. Here's what this does. You're getting *almost* the same benefits of the 15-year loan, while still giving yourself some breathing room in case, for a time, you're not able to make the full payment. Say you lose your job and can't find a new one for several months. I sleep better at night knowing that I don't have to pay as much as I actually do pay for my monthly mortgage in case any financial emergency befalls me.

In a sense, this is like forced, automatic savings. You'll be building equity much faster, and you'll be shaving off tens of thousands of dollars in interest payments over the life of the loan. Really, the more you can pay toward your mortgage, assuming your other budgeting areas have been wisely addressed, the better. If there's one thing I hate, it's paying interest. It's basically my main directive in life to pay off mortgages as soon as humanly possible. You will still get a lower interest rate on a 15-year loan, so this will give you a slight edge in total interest paid, but the difference is negligible enough for me that it's worth it for that extra security I gain from a 30-year loan. We'll get more into extra payments in a bit, but until then, just know that the choice between a 15-year and 30-year loan comes with pros and cons, and it's up to you to decide whether that extra security is worth paying more in interest. If you're super comfortable with the 15-year payment, by all means, go that route.

CLOSING COSTS

You've discussed loan types and terms with your lender, selected the best one for your situation, and now you're ready to get things rolling. Your lender will provide you with a legally required loan estimate form, which clearly lists all the costs and terms of the loan. It will tell you whether or not certain expenses can increase, whether there's a prepayment penalty, what will be included in your escrow account, which services you can and can't shop for, as well as your projected monthly payment and estimated closing costs. These forms make it very easy to compare offers between lenders, and clearly see the full costs of the loan.

There's no way around many closing costs, but several items can be negotiable. These include the loan origination/underwriting fees, application fees, title insurance, homeowners insurance, real estate commissions, and discount points, which are basically prepaid interest to lower your interest rate. Usually, in the non-negotiable category are property taxes, appraisals, flood certifications, recording fees, and most expenses related to taxes. There are many other possible closing costs, so if you have any questions, ask your lender to clarify for you. We will be getting into more of this in the final two steps.

YOUR MONTHLY PAYMENT: PITI

By this point in the process, you probably have a pretty good idea what your monthly mortgage payment will be. That single payment will go toward four different categories: principal, interest, taxes, and insurance. Taxes and insurance are often not included in some estimates and calculations, so it's important to understand how these work together.

First up, principal and interest. If you borrow $200,000, your principal is $200,000. A portion of your monthly payment is allocated to pay this down, but it's probably way less than you think. Especially during the first half of your loan term, the majority of your payment is actually going toward interest, the first I in PITI. Yuck. The best way to hedge this unpleasant reality is to make those extra payments that you designate to go toward your principal. This will shave both time and interest off your loan, but more on that later.

The 'TI' in PITI stands for taxes and insurance. The tax portion of this is an amount set aside to pay your property taxes, which vary county to county. While your annual property tax can vary widely by where you live in the country, in most places, you can generally expect that they will increase each year, if only slightly. This is important to know, as this can actually change your monthly mortgage payment. Here's why. The business entity that you send your monthly mortgage payment to is called your mortgage servicer. They collect your payment, and set aside a portion each month to be able to cover your annual tax bill when the time comes. It's actually pretty handy that you don't have to worry about it. You're essentially paying 1/12th of your tax bill each month. Your servicer will hold that money in an escrow account (basically just an account managed by your servicer) until it's tax time once a year. They'll then withdraw the money they've been setting aside, pay your tax bill, and if there's any excess, they will credit your account. This would make next year's payment slightly lower. Conversely, if taxes have gone up and there won't be enough in escrow to cover your bill, your monthly payment will be adjusted upwards to incorporate the higher costs.

This is also how your home insurance works in most cases. You'll be able to shop around for your home insurance, even bundle it with your car insurance if that gets you a better deal, but in most cases, your mortgage servicer pays that bill for you as well. If you've overpaid to escrow, and your yearly home insurance premium is lower than they expected, you'll be credited and your monthly payment will be slightly lower. And vice versa if the premium is higher than expected.

Home insurance is important to both you and your lender. The lender wants to protect her collateral, and the homeowner wants to protect his property and equity. Most insurance policies will cover hazards, such as your home burning down (don't walk away from the toaster, ok?), and liability if, for example, someone slips on your icy sidewalks. You may also be required to pay flood and/or earthquake insurance, depending on where you live.

SOME FYIS

Speaking of mortgage servicers, you should know that it's possible your loan can be sold at any time. This will not affect any of your loan terms, but it will change from whom you receive bills, and who you talk to if you have any problems. It's technically not a very big deal, but I was pretty annoyed when my loan got sold, as I had a difficult time with the new servicer's customer service. This is less likely to happen if you have a large percentage as down payment, but it's something to be aware of, so you can avoid freaking out if it happens to you.

Once you've officially applied for your loan, it is very wise to avoid any other credit or loan inquiries while everything is processing. If you make any big account changes, or apply for a car loan, this can really throw a wrench in the underwriting process and will likely cause delays. If an emergency comes up, please speak with your lender before you do anything, if at all possible.

Whew, ok, we're on the home stretch now. (I'm sorry, but that pun will probably come up again.) Now that you have a pretty darn accurate monthly payment that includes principal, interest, taxes, and insurance (PITI), I want you to pull out that hypothetical budget you made, and plug that payment in. How does that feel? Is your budget still workable? Are you comfortable? Real talk here: if you're not feeling good about it, it's not too late to back out at this point. Yes, you would probably lose your earnest money, and that doesn't feel great. But we're talking about fifteen to thirty years of debt here. A payment you can't actually afford is going to cause big trouble down the road. Not just the risk of default and foreclosure, but the stress and strain that this can put on your psyche and your relationships is just not worth it; I've seen this firsthand many times. Just know that walking away is an option, albeit a sticky one, right up until closing. But if you followed step two carefully, you likely have nothing to worry about—you know what you can and can't afford.

PAYING OFF YOUR MORTGAGE EARLY

This is the part where I grab your shoulders, look you in the eyes, and say earnestly, "Reader? You should make extra mortgage payments." Here's why.

Say you bought a $250,000 home with 5% down (that would be $12,500). Your interest rate is 3% and your monthly payment would be approximately $1000. This is easier to calculate without taxes and insurance, so for these purposes, this payment does not include them. But just be aware that the TI portion of your total PITI payment is often roughly 20% on top of your principal and interest payment.

In this scenario, let's say you cancel one restaurant meal per month, and instead of spending that $20 on burgers and dessert, you pay it toward your loan principal. That doesn't sound like a lot, right? Twenty bucks a month? I hear you saying, "Sam, that's hardly going to make a difference." But wait, dear naysaying reader! What if I told you this would shave an entire **year** off your 30-year mortgage? What if I told you this would save you a whopping $4,305 in interest?! Would you go bananas?? You should!

This is my very favorite part of this entire book. I love sharing this news with people. When we're dealing with such long loan terms, little differences each month can add up to enormous amounts over the life of the loan. This is why I've been stressing that you don't want to overextend yourself above your budget. This is why I've been saying to pay any extra that you can. If you can only manage it some months and not others? Good for you! Every dollar counts!

If that example gets your heart pumping, wait until you see this one. Let's assume the same mortgage terms as the one above, except this time you decide to make bi-weekly payments. Most lenders will set this up for you to happen automatically if you ask them. Now, instead of making a payment of $1000 once per month, you'll be making a payment of $500 every two weeks. That sounds just about the same, right? Wrong! There are 52 weeks in the year, which means that you'll be making 26 payments. When you add that up, you'll basically be making one additional payment of $1000 each year, except you'll hardly notice it. (Twenty-six payments times $500 per payment equals $13,000 paid per year; versus twelve payments of $1000 equals $12,000 per year.)

Are you ready to hear how much time and money this will save you? I can honestly hardly contain myself. By making this easy switch, that will feel almost exactly the same to you on a monthly basis, you will be knocking three and a half *years* off your 30-year loan term, and saving yourself about $16,500 in interest over the life of the loan! Did you hear that?? Over sixteen *thousand* dollars, just by making a hardly noticeable change to your payment plan. This is something I want to shout from the rooftops. And if one extra payment per year can save you that much time and money, can you even imagine if you managed to pay even more than that? Well, you don't have to imagine it, because I'll be listing my favorite calculator in the resource section for you to play around with these numbers and easily figure out how much you can save in your situation. Be careful though, as you might turn into a giant nerd and find yourself treating this more like a game to see how much time and interest you can shave off of your loan.

I want you to keep this perspective as you work through your budget and pick the right home for you and your family. Paying extra down payment, extra monthly payments, fighting hard for the best interest rate by improving your credit, negotiating where you can—all these things will save you So. Much. Dang. Money. Yes, it will take more effort, and certainly more time, but if you can keep this longer-term, zoomed out perspective, you'll be so happy you did!

INSPECTION, APPRAISALS, INSURANCE, OH MY!

The end is in sight! You've found your house, made an offer, and had it accepted. But there are still a few more hurdles to clear before closing. Between having your offer accepted and actually closing on the house, you typically have a few weeks to have the property inspected, select your insurance providers, and generally make sure every last T is crossed and every I is dotted.

By this point, you might be ready to just hurry up and close on the house, so you can move in and start your new life as a homeowner. I don't blame you one bit, but these are important steps, and they deserve your time and attention. Done right, they can save you thousands of dollars in the long run, not to mention significant stress and aggravation. So as tempting as it might be to rush through these steps as mere formalities, I urge you to take your time and go through each of them carefully. In this chapter, we'll discuss:

- Property inspection
- Appraisal
- Insurance
- Final Walkthrough
- Closing disclosure

Since the first step is usually to have the house inspected, let's start there!

HOME INSPECTION

What is a home inspection? Simply put, you pay a professional to check out the property and make sure there aren't any potentially expensive issues that could come back to bite you later. This is where we get down and dirty (maybe literally) about the shape your house is *really* in.

A home inspection was likely one of your contingencies in your offer, so the purchase price isn't set in stone until after it's done. You'll want to get the inspection done quickly so that you have enough time to negotiate any problems that might come up. You also want to make sure there is sufficient time for the other steps you'll need to take before closing.

Even if your lender doesn't require a home inspection (although the vast majority do), it's well worth the relatively minor cost to ensure that there aren't any unpleasant surprises after you move in. If the A/C isn't working or the furnace has given up the ghost, you'll want to know that *before* you sign on the dotted line, not after!

Your agent likely has someone he can recommend (and may even set it up for you), but if you know a licensed inspector you trust, go with him! If not, look for local inspectors with good online reviews who are able to do the inspection and provide a report within a reasonable timeframe. On average, a home inspection will cost around $325, though this will vary depending on where you are.

Typically, an inspector will check the following:

- Electrical, plumbing, and HVAC systems to make sure they're in good working order
- Major appliances that are being left with the house to be sure they are running properly
- Roof, foundation, walls, and crawlspaces to be sure they are structurally sound
- Exterior features such as doors, decks and driveways
- Interior features such as staircases, windows and garages

Allow two to three hours for the inspection, and plan on being present the entire time. Don't be afraid to ask your inspector questions and point out any areas of specific concern to you. You're making a big purchase, and you have the right to know as much about the property as possible!

This is also a good chance for you to get familiar with your new home-to-be. Take note of where you can find the electrical box, the furnace emergency switch, and the water main shutoff. Trust me on this—it's better to learn where they are now rather than when a pipe bursts!

When your inspector is done, you'll get a full report detailing any problems he finds. While it's your inspector's job to point out areas of concern, you may need to go a step further and hire an expert to follow up and figure out the full scope of a specific problem. This is extra time and money, of course, but it's worth it to know how expensive the problem could be and how quickly it needs to be addressed. If your inspector suggests hiring a specialist to take a closer look at something, listen to him!

If the inspection turns up problems that you'd like to have fixed before taking ownership, talk to your real estate agent and enlist his help in negotiating with the seller. Generally speaking, you'll want to focus on repairs that will be expensive or that could pose safety hazards if not addressed; relatively minor and cosmetic issues don't make for worthwhile delays and are usually easy enough for you to take care of yourself. Depending on the issues your inspector finds, you can ask the seller to make repairs, ask the seller to give you cash or credit at closing so that you can take care of them yourself, or lower the selling price.

It's rare to find problems that are so extensive that it makes more sense to call off the sale altogether, but it can happen. Obviously, it's disappointing when it does, but you're significantly better off discovering problems now, rather than after you move in and the roof collapses! (Don't worry; that hardly ever happens!)

The majority of the time, of course, the results won't be that dramatic. In fact, you may not find any serious issues, which, of course, is a good thing. It's still money well spent, as the inspection will let you know what to expect from your new home over the long term (like when you'll need to start thinking about a new roof, for example), as well as give you peace of mind with your purchase.

Make the most of this step by asking lots of questions and reading your inspector's report thoroughly. It's one of the best investments of time and money you can make in your new home-to-be!

APPRAISAL

You know what you are willing to pay, but do you know what your home-to-be is really *worth*? Even if you're happy with the price you have offered for the home, your lender may not be.

She will require an official appraisal of the home as a way of protecting the bank's investment (the loan they're giving you) in the property. Unless you're paying cash for your home, there's likely no way around this cost. But even if you disagree that it should be mandatory, it's still a good idea to get a professional opinion on the property's value to ensure that you're not paying too much.

The appraiser is a trained professional with a license and certification who will inspect the home, inside and out. She may take several hours at the house to do this, but some get in and out rather quickly. More work goes on behind the scenes, so don't be too concerned if your appraiser doesn't spend a great deal of time at the actual property. Once she gets back to her office, she will be taking market trends and recent sales of similar homes in the area into consideration in order to come up with a value for the home. And if that value is equal to or more than what you have offered to pay? Great! Everything can proceed as planned.

If it is less than your offer, however, your lender may refuse to loan you the full amount you have requested. After all, if you default on the loan, they get stuck with the property; and they don't want to risk getting stuck with something that's worth less than they paid for it!

Assuming you followed step 5, you have likely listed an appraisal as a contingency in your offer, so if the appraisal is lower than expected, you can withdraw the offer without losing your earnest money. However, if you really love the house, you do still have some options:

- You can use the appraisal to negotiate a lower price with the seller.
- You could hire a different appraiser for a second opinion (which, of course, will cost you more).
- You can make the case to the appraiser that the property is worth more than his report stated. If there have been a number of short sales and foreclosures in your area, for instance, they can make it seem as though properties are worth less than they really are.

An appraisal typically costs $300-$600, but they may cost even more in metropolitan areas or for large properties. I have never heard of one costing more than $1000, but I wouldn't be surprised if someone could top that. Nearly all costs associated with purchasing a home vary significantly from area to area, so ask your lender to give you an estimate, if you'd like to find out more before you find yourself in this stage. Take note that your lender will choose the appraiser and you, the loan applicant, will pay for it. The payment is usually thrown in with all your other closing costs, which we'll discuss in the next step.

HOMEOWNER'S INSURANCE

Your lender will also require insurance on the property—and of course, you'll want this too! Homeowner's insurance covers your property in the event of damage or destruction from fire, storms, vandalism, and other disasters. It also covers your possessions in the event of theft or destruction. If you lose all your furniture and clothing in a fire, for example, your policy should reimburse you for these, as well as for the replacement of your home, usually up to 50-70% of its value. If your possessions are worth more than this—if you own expensive jewelry, art, or antiques, for example—you may want to ask about additional coverage in the form of an itemized schedule or a rider.

Most standard homeowner insurance policies do *not* cover floods and earthquakes. However, if you live in a flood- or earthquake-prone area, your lender will likely require that you are fully covered through an additional rider. Outbuildings on the property, such as free standing garages or barns, may not be covered by the primary policy, so be sure to ask about additional coverage for those.

Remember that the cost of rebuilding your home might be substantially more than what you owe on your mortgage. Base your coverage on what it would take to rebuild your home in the event of a total loss, such as a fire, and not simply on market value.

Although the lender requires you to get insurance, you get to pick your insurance carrier, so this is another opportunity to shop around. You might consider bundling with whoever provides your car insurance for an extra discount, but it's a good idea to check out other local firms as well. You'll want to apply my same advice from step 3 by getting a quote from one agent, asking if a second can beat it, and so on until you've contacted three or four insurance agents and received the best possible rates. Don't feel bad pitting them against each other and negotiating as much as you can. You can save hundreds, if not thousands, by doing this extra legwork, and it really won't take you too much extra time. You'll need to provide proof of insurance at or before closing, so don't wait on this!

TITLE INSURANCE

Your lender will require title insurance as well. This is to protect you and your lender in the event that there are legal claims against the property.

How could this happen? If, for example, the previous owners ignored a weed citation and accumulated late fees on the fine, you might wake up one day with a letter from the city telling you that there's a lien on your house and ordering *you* to pay the full amount; even if you have been taking good care of the weeds since you moved in! Same thing if the previous owner didn't pay all their taxes, or the home was used as collateral for an unpaid loan, or there's a pending lawsuit, or a long-lost heir to the property shows up... You get the picture.

As unlikely as some of these things may seem, they've all happened at one time or another, so you (and your lender) would hate for it to happen to your property. Such title problems can make for messy and expensive legal proceedings, and in the worst-case scenario, could result in you losing your home.

Before you close, your lender will insist on having a title research company check your property to make sure that there are no outstanding liens or claims on the property. Hopefully, the title research won't turn up any red flags, but even if it doesn't, a policy will still be required in case those issues simply haven't surfaced yet (remember that long-lost heir!).

This is where title insurance comes into play. Title insurance comes in two flavors: a lender's policy, which protects the lender up to the amount of money borrowed; and an owner's policy, which protects the owner's interest in the property up to the actual sales price. Your lender will require a loan policy, which will protect his interest in the property, i.e., the amount of the mortgage. As the mortgage is paid off, his interest decreases and is dissolved completely once it is paid off; although you will have already paid for the full policy upfront, so don't expect your payment to get any smaller.

An owner's policy is optional, but it's still a good idea. This policy protects *your* interest in the property for as long as you own it. Even if a title issue arises years from now, you're still covered.

The premium you pay for title insurance is almost always a one-time payment at closing. You can expect it to cost around $550-$4000, depending on whether you opt for an owner's policy in addition to the required lender's policy. This is yet another area where you can save big by shopping around. All those title agents will usually negotiate with you for your business; and often, they'll even throw in the owner's policy for a fraction of the cost of the loan policy—or even for free in some cases. The good news is that these are one-time costs, not ongoing fees.

FINAL WALKTHROUGH

Although it's sometimes treated as little more than a formality, the final walkthrough is your last chance to inspect the property before you officially close on it. It usually takes place just a day or two before closing, and you may be tempted to skip it or rush through it, so you can just *buy the darn house already!* But please don't. This is your chance to make sure that everything is in order and that any repairs you've requested have been made. You can also check to make sure that the repairs themselves haven't caused other problems, such as debris that workers failed to clean up.

Your real estate agent will go with you and should be able to guide you on what to look out for, but here's a quick list for your own reference.

Be sure that:

- The seller has removed all personal belongings
- The surrounding property is clear of seller's possessions
- There is no debris in the yard or the house
- All agreed-upon repairs have been made
- All systems and appliances included in the sale are still on the premises and in working condition
- All fixtures are in place (unless otherwise agreed, things like light fixtures, molding, etc. are considered part of the house and should stay with the property)

If there are any issues, your agent can help you work with the seller to get them addressed before closing.

THE CLOSING DISCLOSURE

We're so close to the finish line now—hang in there! (I'll spare you more home-stretch puns.) We have one more step before we get to the all-important closing day: the closing disclosure. There's nothing particularly fascinating about this document, but the good news is that it's usually short, just a few pages, and shouldn't take too much more of your time or energy.

So, what is it and when do you get it? Once the walkthrough is complete, you'll get your official closing disclosure from your lender. It will include the final terms of the mortgage, your exact PITI monthly payment, and your total closing costs. It's basically a summary of all your costs, present and ongoing, related to your home purchase.

Your lender is required to give it to you at least three days before closing so that you have adequate time to examine it. Double check to be sure that your loan amount, down payment, interest rate, address, and even the spelling of your name are all correct. If you find *any* errors at all, contact your lender as quickly as possible to get them resolved. Likewise, if there is anything you don't understand, be sure to ask your lender or your real estate agent. Once it all looks good, you're ready to close, baby!

FINAL THOUGHTS

You've made sure there are no issues with your home that could be a hazard to your safety or wallet later on. You've lined up insurance to protect your investment. You've done one final inspection of the property. And you've made sure that you and your lender are on the same page about your obligations.

Sit down and take a nice, deep breath. The hard stuff is out of the way, and we are now truly on the home stretch (you didn't really think I could leave that alone, did you?). Now it's time for the actual closing. Limber up your writing hand because you're going to be signing a *lot* of documents!

8

CLOSING: IT'S NOT AS INTIMIDATING AS YOU THINK
(AND YOU MIGHT JUST GET YOURSELF A FANCY PEN!)

A re you getting excited? You've cleared all the hurdles so far, and most of the hard work is behind you (well, until it's time to unpack all those boxes). Don't get complacent yet, though! We still need to close on the house. It's not particularly difficult or even all that time-consuming, but there are a few things I want you to be aware of, so we can be sure it all goes smoothly.

When you made an offer on the home, an estimated date for closing was included. This date could be several weeks or even months from when your offer was accepted (the average is 41 days). The actual date will likely be solidified between your agent, your lender, and the title agent to make sure everyone has enough time to complete the tasks we've discussed in previous chapters. So, let's talk about closing and what to expect!

This is the day you will officially be the owner of your new home. It will probably take place at a title company's office. Sometimes the seller is present, sometimes not. In theory, *you* don't even need to be present, as long as you have someone there who's authorized to legally represent you. But I'm going to assume that you'll show up—because this is the day all your hard work comes to fruition!

In most cases, some or all of the following people will be there with you: an escrow officer, a mortgage professional, an attorney (if applicable—see the next section), a home inspector, a title agent, your real estate agent, and of course, your spouse/co-signer.

There are a couple of caveats I wanted to mention just in case, though you probably weren't going to do these things anyway: do *not* make any drastic changes that could affect your credit score (like buying $15,000 worth of furniture for your new home), and do *not* quit your job before closing. The mortgage company's underwriter will do one last check of your credit and employment status, perhaps even as close as 24 hours before closing. You might even be asked to sign a document at closing promising that your employment status hasn't changed. You've come this far—don't risk your home with a silly mistake!

And now, the reason you probably purchased this book, perhaps the most important part of the entire process: how to get a really nice pen at closing. I'll keep it short and sweet. When I closed on my first home, some friends had closed a few months before at the same title company, and they each got these beautiful, heavy pens from the company. These weren't normal pens, ok? These were pens that a broke college student like me had never even held. The heft, the luxurious ink flow; they were pen perfection. Suffice it to say, I get excited about silly little things, and I was really looking forward to getting our own super pens at closing.

So we sat down at the desk, all the closing professionals around us, and on the table for us to sign all our documents were these run-of-the-mill, black ink, plastic pens. So lame. I made a tongue-in-cheek comment to my husband about how devastated I was, but I have to admit, I was actually a little disappointed. Our real estate agent overheard me and said, "You guys wanted nice pens?"

I waved my hand flippantly and said it wasn't a big deal. But she flagged down the title agent and said that we'd been told there would be nice pens. The staff fumbled around, saying they thought they had just run out, but that they would check, while I died of embarrassment. I don't like making a fuss. But lo and behold, there were two pens left, which they forked over to us. Reader, these pens were so beautiful, I quickly forgot my embarrassment. Just one more reason to pick an assertive real estate agent who will get you what you want! So, if you play your cards right, you, too, might be walking away with a new house AND your new favorite pen.

And guess what? You're going to want that nice pen, because oh boy, are you going to be signing a lot of papers. Seriously. It will probably take a couple of hours just to get through everything. But I'm getting a little ahead of myself. Let's back up a bit and talk about what to expect and how to prepare for closing.

DO YOU NEED A LAWYER?

As with many of life's questions, the answer to this is a big fat "maybe." In large part, it depends on where you're closing. At the time of writing this book, 21 states and the District of Columbia required that you have a lawyer physically present at your closing. Check with your real estate agent to see if you need one.

Even if you're not legally mandated to have one, you can certainly hire one, if you would like that extra peace of mind. It's an extra expense, but it might be worth it to have an expert look over all your documents before signing, particularly if the property in question has any unique concerns. Your lawyer will make sure that deeds, insurance documents, and payoff letters are all accurate and finalized before you sign them and will explain to you what each one means.

If you need or want a lawyer, you'll want to look into hiring one well before the actual closing day. You can ask your real estate agent for recommendations or look for one in your area who specializes in real estate.

SCAMS

I hate even having to write about this, but I'd be remiss if I didn't at least mention it. The unfortunate fact is that there are con artists out there who prey specifically on people who are about to close on their homes. These scammers know that there are large sums of money involved. They also know that since most of us don't buy homes very often, we aren't usually very familiar with the process and may not recognize the warning signs until it's too late.

The good news is that it's statistically very unlikely to happen to you. The bad news is that mortgage and closing scams have risen exponentially over the past few years—so it's more likely to happen than it used to be. So this isn't your run-of-the-mill paranoia; it's a real issue, and it's smart to be on the lookout for it.

So how does a scam work, and how do you avoid being a victim? Typically, you'll get an email from someone posing as your real estate agent or settlement agent with last-minute changes for wiring or electronically transferring your closing costs. These scams can be incredibly sophisticated and may involve emails, websites, and even phone numbers that really, *really* look like they belong to people and companies you trust. Scammers can even use "spoofing" software that allows them to make calls and send emails using real numbers and addresses of people you know. A clever hacker may have read your email correspondence and may even be able to throw personal details into their correspondence that only you would know.

Scary stuff, right? So how do you protect yourself?

1. Make sure to get contact information directly from the professionals involved in your closing (your real estate agent, settlement agent, mortgage company representative, and so forth) and save it in a safe place.

2. Understand your closing process. It's *highly* unlikely that there will be a last-minute emergency requiring you to wire funds or do anything with your money other than what you've already been told to do.

3. Be leery of last-minute changes to the closing process, *especially* when it involves your money. Scammers prey on the sense of panic they create with messages like "URGENT" or "ACT NOW OR YOU MAY LOSE YOUR HOME," so be especially wary of messages designed to pressure you into acting quickly.

4. Do not click any links in suspicious emails or download attachments, and *never* send sensitive financial information (like credit card or bank account numbers, passwords, etc.) via email.

5. Be wary of phone conversations. You may get a call that looks like it's coming from your real estate agent's office or your mortgage company telling you they have important information for you and asking you to confirm your identity first by handing

over personal identifying details like your social security number. Hang up the phone and call one of your trusted parties on a number you know is theirs.

6. If someone sends you new instructions about how or where to send your money, contact your representative over the phone or in person. Use *only* the contact information you've saved; do not reply to any suspicious emails or phone messages.

Once you have wired money to another bank account, it can be very difficult to get it back, but if you think you've been scammed, contact your bank asap and tell them what happened. Also, file a complaint with the FBI and IRS Criminal Investigation.

As I said above, this probably won't happen—but I need you to know that it *could* happen. Forewarned is forearmed and all that, right? And now that you know what to be on the lookout for, you're way less likely to run into this kind of trouble and you can proceed with confidence.

WHAT AND WHOM TO BRING WITH YOU

You've hired your lawyer (or not), you've dodged the scams, now it's time to close! As I mentioned, you don't *technically* need to be present for closing, but you do need an authorized representative there on your behalf. I strongly suggest being there in person if you can, but if you can't, look into hiring a real estate lawyer as soon as you can to represent you.

So assuming you and your co-signer plan to show up in person, now what? What do you actually *do*? And what should you bring with you? Let's have a quick look at what to expect and how to prepare.

Your agent should let you know about any specific items to bring, but this is generally what you should plan on having with you:

- Photo identification (note: if you've recently changed your name for marriage or any other reason, your I.D. needs to match the name that will appear on the property's title and mortgage)
- A second form of identification with your name but not necessarily your photo
- Certified or cashier's check for any amount that hasn't been deducted from the sales price (in some cases, you might be instructed to wire your closing costs)
- Income statements (pay stubs, W-2 forms)
- Asset statements (bank accounts, investments)
- Proof of homeowners insurance
- Your home inspection reports
- Copy of your contract with the seller
- Any paperwork the bank required to approve your loan

If applicable:

- Divorce decree
- Child support or alimony information that proves you're up to date with payments
- Bankruptcy papers

Bring it all in a folder and be prepared to hand it over when asked.

WHAT TO EXPECT

You've walked into the title office with your I.D. and a thick folder of papers, plus any co-signers in tow. You may be invited immediately to a conference room to sit at a big table with whomever else has already arrived. You'll be at that table for the next couple of hours to sign papers, so you'll probably be offered some water. But since you read this book, you probably brought your own water bottle and all you care about is the new pen. Eye on the prize.

Now, this is important: there's SO much paperwork to go through (probably 50 to 100 pages) at this stage that it's tempting to just sign wherever you're told and check out on reading each page. I totally get that. But don't do it! Take the time to read each page and understand what you're signing—you're making a major financial commitment, after all! I'm not talking about pouring over each and every word on every document; you don't want to be there past midnight. But don't be intimidated if you want to pause to read more thoroughly or ask any questions of anyone there. You're surrounded by experts whose job it is to explain what each document means, so take advantage of that.

WHAT AM I SIGNING, ANYWAY?

Although the exact documents required may vary depending on state and local laws, they break down into two broad categories: documents that transfer the property from the seller to you, and documents of agreement between you and your lender. You'll also sign a host of affidavits swearing to your identity and that any information you provide is true to the best of your knowledge. You can ask your closing agent for a list of documents specific to your situation, but here's what you can expect at virtually all closings:

TITLE DOCUMENTS

Title documents record your right to your home; technically, you won't *own* the property until you've completely paid off your mortgage, but having the title gives you the right to it. As I mentioned in the last chapter, your lender should have appointed a title research company to make sure that the title is clear, so there shouldn't be any surprises here. You're basically just confirming that the title is as you expected.

CLOSING DISCLOSURE

I mentioned this in the last chapter: it's the document you get from your lender summarizing all the costs associated with your mortgage. You should actually have received this three days before closing to review, but now you get to sign it!

MORTGAGE PROMISSORY NOTE

Sometimes called the mortgage note or just "the note," this document contains all the details of your loan, such as the total amount of the loan, the interest rate, the term of the loan, and even where to send payments. When you sign it, you're legally promising to repay your lender according to the terms of the note, so read it carefully to be sure it matches up with your understanding of the terms.

THE MORTGAGE / DEED OF TRUST / SECURITY INSTRUMENT

The deed of trust gives the lender the legal right to foreclose on your home should you fail to honor the terms of the mortgage *note*. Pay special attention to the "fill-in-the-blank" portions that have been personalized for you and your situation to make sure the information is accurate.

THE DEED (FOR PROPERTY TRANSFER)

(I know, I know—all these overlapping names are starting to get confusing. Hang tight; this is mostly just for your own information.) Not to be confused with the deed of trust above, this deed is the document that transfers ownership of the property from the seller to YOU (yay!). In most cases, the seller will have already signed it and had it notarized. Review it carefully to be sure all the information is correct. After closing, the deed will go to your county to be recorded, creating a public record with you as the owner.

INITIAL ESCROW DISCLOSURE STATEMENT

Typically, you'll bundle your mortgage payments with property tax, PMI, and insurance premiums all into one monthly payment. Your lender will put the extra money aside in an escrow account and use it to pay your taxes and insurance on your behalf. By signing this document, you agree to the terms of the escrow agreement.

TRANSFER TAX DECLARATION

This is required in states and localities with a property transfer tax. You and the seller both sign declarations disclosing the purchase price and calculating the tax.

So, sign, sign, sign, stand up, shake hands with everyone, and congratulations—you're a homeowner! You probably want to go rest your signature hand in your new home, but not so fast. Assuming you haven't made any rent-back arrangements with the seller, you'll probably still need to wait until your county officially records the title.

WAIT A SEC, BACK UP. WHAT'S A RENT-BACK ARRANGEMENT?

This is worth mentioning, as it's a fairly common occurrence. A rent-back arrangement gives the sellers extra time to live in the home after closing—as your tenants, basically. It's a boon to sellers who might not have been able to close on *their* new house yet, and it can make your offer stronger if you're willing to play ball. Besides, having someone pay you a month or two of rent might be a nice bonus after shelling out all that money at closing.

It does come with drawbacks, though. For one, if you let the sellers stay longer than 60 days, you may be in violation of your agreement that the property will be owner-occupied. For another, you assume the responsibilities of a landlord as long as they're renting from you, meaning you're on call to fix any problems that come up. And of course, you can't actually move in until your seller-tenants have moved out, so it may or may not be a practical choice for you, depending on your situation. Obviously, any rent-back arrangements should be made well before closing, and you should check with your lender before finalizing any agreement like this.

WHY IS RECORDING THE DEED IMPORTANT?

Having the deed officially recorded is important because until it's done, the seller could sell the property to someone else (highly unlikely but theoretically possible), you wouldn't be able to sell or refinance your home, and you could be liable for any liens or judgments that the title search didn't turn up. Yikes, right?

Recording the deed can happen very quickly, perhaps the same day as closing, or, frustratingly, several days after. This should be spelled out in your contract, and you should be aware of when you'll get access to the house before closing, but if you have any doubt, ask!

For a host of reasons, you can't move in until it is legally your home, but once that title is recorded and you've picked up the keys from the seller's agent, gather your moving buddies, the home is yours!

MOVING IN!

You've got your keys in one hand and the title documents in the other; now the fun begins! Even though you've signed off legally, there are still things you need to do to ensure a smooth transition to your new home. I didn't want to leave you hanging, so here's a list of helpful to-do's for before and after closing that will help ensure a smooth transition to homeownership. A lot of these are common sense, and you may have already thought of some of them, but in the excitement of closing, they're easy to overlook.

Make copies of your closing documents and keep them in a safe place

Yes, your county clerk should have a record of the sale, but it's wise to know where your documents are, to have back-ups, and a safe place to keep them. Consider a fireproof safe (a good investment anyway) or a safe deposit box at your bank.

Schedule your moving company

You've hopefully booked your moving company (or moving buddies) in advance, but now is the time to confirm exactly when and where they're going. Take any big restoration projects into account when setting the date. If you need to refinish your floors, for example, make sure the furniture doesn't get moved in until they're done.

Hook up your utilities

It's worth calling your internet/cable provider even before closing, so that you can get someone out to the house to set you up as soon as possible after you move in (who can live without internet?!). You can begin the process of switching over the gas bill, water bill, and electric bill to your name even before you move in (in fact you should, or you may find yourself moving into a very cold, dark house). Simply call each of your local utility companies to ask what needs to be done to put the bills in your name. While you're at it, find out what your options for trash and recycling pick up are. Most of these services can be set up very quickly.

Contact the school district, if you have kids

Let them know you've moved into the district and ask how to register your child(ren).

Change your address

This is another task you can get a jumpstart on even before moving in. Start by calling your local DMV to find out what you'll need to do to update your driver's license and be sure to let your employer know you're moving. Move on to updating credit card companies, banks, doctors, and other service providers. Don't forget to let your auto insurance company know you've moved, especially if you've moved to a new state. Your premiums and coverage could be affected. And a pro tip: when ordering online, double-check to make sure your old address has been removed from each store's system.

Forward your mail

Check out www.moversguide.usps.com for instructions on having your mail forwarded from your old address. Make sure to set it so that it begins arriving at your new home on or after your move-in date.

Reset security codes and change the locks

There's really no way to know who may have copies of the keys to your house or the codes to your security systems, so changing them is a smart safety measure. You'll need to make an appointment with a locksmith for a time that you can physically be at the home. And while you're thinking of it, get a lockbox and put a spare key in it, in case you get locked out.

Check smoke and carbon monoxide alarms

This is something to do as soon as you move in. Make sure they're all present and working. It's a good idea to pop in fresh batteries as well.

Install fire extinguishers

Along the same lines, make sure you have a fire extinguisher in the kitchen and each additional floor.

Find the circuit box, emergency shut-offs, and appliance manuals

Hopefully, you located the circuit box, water and gas shut-offs, and furnace emergency switch when you did the home inspection. If you didn't, now is the time to find them, and make anyone else in your household aware of them as well. While you're at it, make sure you have manuals for any large appliances that came with the house. If they've disappeared, you can usually download them from the manufacturer's website.

Go over your inspection report

Hopefully, the previous owner has dealt with any major issues, but if there are still repairs to be done, list them out and make a schedule for dealing with them.

Research tax deductions

You may be able to claim the cost of points paid, mortgage interest, PMI, and even some home improvements as tax deductions. Talk to your accountant.

Introduce yourself to the neighbors

If your neighborhood isn't conducive to just running into people, you might have to make the effort to knock on some doors and let people know who you are. This is as practical as it is neighborly. Don't assume that your new neighbors know that the old owners moved out. If you take the time to introduce yourself, you won't have to worry about them wondering if you belong there! Maybe you'll even make a friend who will keep an eye on your house while you're out of town.

And of course: Celebrate!

You own your own house! Take some time to celebrate. Whether it's a fancy housewarming party or a casual barbeque with friends and family, this is your chance to show off your new purchase, accept well wishes, and enjoy your new home. If you're feeling adventurous, invite some of your new neighbors and get to know them.

Give yourself a pat on the back. You've earned it. Congratulations, and welcome home!

CONCLUSION

You did it! Congratulations! Cue the triumphant fanfare! Buying a new home can be an extremely stressful process, even with the best laid plans, but hopefully by employing the tips from this book, you have saved yourself any unnecessary cost and hassle. And now you get to kick back in your new living room, crank up the volume on your favorite movie, and enjoy all the benefits that come with homeownership.

You've been through a lot. Once you got the full picture of this process in chapter one, you moved on to perhaps the toughest step: building your financial foundation. Maybe you had to take a few extra months to get your budget in order and save enough money for your down payment and closing costs. You figured out how big of a monthly payment you could actually afford and tested it out in your hypothetical, post-purchase budget. Maybe you even took those months to pay off more debt and discover an incredible first-time homebuyer program in your area. Aren't you so glad that you took this time? The tens of thousands of dollars that will stay in your pocket as the years pass will certainly thank you!

Once you felt like your finances were secure and you had a solid game plan, you shopped around and found a fantastic real estate agent and lender. Sure, you made him match a different lender's rates and played a little hardball with him, but now you guys are peas in a pod! Since you had already gathered all your documents, getting pre-approved was a cinch and you were ready to shop for your home in what felt like no time.

Remember when you were deciding what type of house to buy? Wasn't that more fun than you thought it would be? Maybe you opted for the single-family unit with the white picket fence, or maybe you wanted that modern condo with the beautiful pool and free monthly massage. I really hope you enjoy that massage; I mean that. After considering all your life circumstances, you probably feel fantastic about the home you chose.

And remember when you made your offer on that home? Man, weren't you nervous? But you had your knowledgeable agent with you, and she knew what kind of offer would work for your local market, and what contingencies you should include, so you were really more excited than nervous. You and that seller sure had some back and forth over whether or not the washer and dryer would stay with the house, but aren't you glad you got it sorted?

Ah, and then there was applying for your actual loan. I bet you had a fun time deciding what type of loan to get, once you had considered your down payment, debt-to-income ratio, and credit score. And since you walked in knowing the pros and cons of each, I bet you now feel confident you got the best deal for your situation. I'd love to know whether you picked a 15- or 30-year loan, but since you'll likely be paying additional principal each month anyway, I'm sure you're happy with your choice. And I know it's going to be an amazing day for you when, because of those additional payments, you get to remove your private mortgage insurance early (assuming you went with a conventional loan, of course). If you save even ten dollars by making an extra payment to your loan, I will be so flipping happy for you!

I bet you were getting pretty eager when you were waiting for your appraisal and home inspection to be done. Did your inspector discover the roof would soon collapse? I sure hope not, but you knew what to do if that was the case. Did your appraisal come in for the amount you offered for the home? Since that's more likely than not, I'll guess you probably didn't have any problems there. Did you shop around for title insurance and home insurance? I doubt the title turned up any problems, but I'm so glad you'll get to sleep well at night knowing you're covered no matter what happens. Maybe you don't even remember getting your closing disclosure statement from your lender since you were so excited to do your final walkthrough. Everything probably looked great and you were stretching your signature hand for closing day!

Please tell me you got a nice pen on closing day? Or at least *a* new pen? I suppose since you did get a house out of the deal, it's not a total wash if you missed out on the pen. I bet once you got through that pile of documents at the closing table that some of the excitement of the day had worn off, but then there was that moment. You signed the last one. Let's assume you live in a county that records the sale very quickly, and you were able to go run through your new home, singing, "Take me home, country roads!" the very same day. Wasn't that surreal? You did it! I'm so proud of you!

So what are we to take away from this journey? That you can do hard things if you break it down into smaller steps? That rushing into big financial decisions rarely yields positive outcomes? That preparing yourself from the ground up, working hard and practicing self-control can earn you security and wealth in the long run? Yes to all of the above! I hope that by reading this book, you feel less stressed, more prepared and more confident to continue making wise financial choices throughout your life. You're well on your way as a new homeowner, who purchased a home you could afford and worked hard to save and budget for it. That kind of mindset is a fantastic foundation for long-term financial health, and you'll be enjoying stable homeownership for many decades to come.

Now that you have the tools and knowledge you need, go forth and purchase with confidence! You've just gone from zero to homeowner in eight simple steps, and I'm so glad you allowed me to guide you. If you found this book helpful, I can't even tell you how much I would appreciate a review on Amazon.

Leaving a review will not only help other potential homebuyers find this information, but it would also delight me to no end.

Peace out, you responsible homeowner, you! :)

RESOURCES

Did you think I would forget about all those times I said I would include a resource for you at the end of this book? Well, not to worry, I've got you covered! I'll list these in the order that I mentioned them, along with the corresponding step so you can find what you're looking for more easily.

Step 1 Resources

Let's start with one I didn't actually mention yet. For anyone moving out of state, here's an article with some tips that might help you: https://bit.ly/34AQCL5

And if you're looking for specific rules about buying a home in a particular state, this may not seem all that helpful, but honestly, your best bet is to just use your search engine and type, "how to purchase a home in [your state]." That's what I would do!

Here's a great article with more of an overview of the entire process for you: https://bit.ly/3uJbxpW

Step 2 Resources

We talked a lot about free online calculators to get you started in figuring out how much house you could afford. Here is Dave Ramsey's calculator, that I think is a great place to start, but is on the more conservative side: https://bit.ly/3uHTGPS

Here is another free calculator I also like from Nerd Wallet, a favorite financial blog of mine: https://bit.ly/3yPxk2x

And another from Bankrate, my go-to source for the latest rates and other information, they have a decent calculator as well: https://bit.ly/3g3oVQe

I also mentioned the importance of a budget in the second chapter. I have some other resources for you here, but there are many, many more online.

From Clever Girl Finance, she runs down her favorite budgeting methods and includes free downloads: https://bit.ly/2Tqw9WQ

Nerd Wallet has you covered as well with an extensive list of budgeting options and free templates: https://bit.ly/3g5gow8

To help give you some ideas about what expenses you might expect during the home buying process, check out this helpful article from Rocket Mortgage: https://bit.ly/3uC9jbD

And this article from Investopedia will help your brainstorm sessions, as they cover some of the less obvious costs of homeownership: https://bit.ly/3g32tXn

Here's some more info from Nerd Wallet about down payments: https://bit.ly/3fKZILr

You may want to consider writing up a creditor sheet. This would simply be a no-frills form to help you organize your debt. While there are plenty of templates available online, you'd do just as well to make your own that includes the creditor's name, the amount owed, the interest rate being charged, and how much time you have left on the loan. Easy peasy.

Speaking of credit, here's that link I promised from Dave Ramsey, explaining how to get a mortgage without a credit score. I don't have any personal experience with this technique, so I can't vouch for it, but it could certainly be a resource worth checking out: https://bit.ly/3i73DDV

If you're wanting to improve your credit, which you likely will, here are a couple of resources for you.

From the horse's mouth, FICO: https://bit.ly/2Tutag1

And from one of the credit bureaus: https://bit.ly/3fGCHcJ

Remember how I mentioned that even a 1% difference in your interest rate will equate to a huge difference in total interest paid over the life of the loan? I didn't have a lot of time to go into it, so check out this article here for more info: https://bit.ly/3wVPihJ

And in case you missed it, if you're looking for a place to start when it comes to first-time home buyer programs in your area, you'll want to go here: https://bit.ly/3fIBDoA

Step 3 Resources

Were you wanting some more help deciding what type of mortgage lender to choose? This article from Experian should give you some more guidance on the considerations between a mortgage broker and a bank: https://bit.ly/3ySCbjj

Here's an article detailing more of the benefits of going with a local credit union: https://bit.ly/3wNZOHP

And here's a great breakdown of tips from Nerd Wallet about how to find the best lender: https://bit.ly/34RnwY5

Still not sure if you need a real estate attorney? Check out this article from my favorite legal website, Nolo: https://bit.ly/3vJT8ue

Lastly, if you wanting to know more about how you lender and real estate agent will be paid, check out this article for lenders: https://bit.ly/3vS1QXG

And this one for agents: https://bit.ly/34Ii9dq

Step 4 Resources

Still not sure about the different house types and their pros and cons? Check out these two articles, one from Homes for Heroes: https://bit.ly/2TyArvw

And one from the Mortgage Reports: https://bit.ly/2SQ4Q8j

Step 5 Resources

For more information on making an offer on your home, check out this article from Rocket Mortgage: https://bit.ly/3vOzoWp

Step 6 Resources

Still not sure which loan type is best for you? Bankrate has an excellent resource here: https://bit.ly/3fMwThC

If, as a veteran or surviving spouse, you are looking for more information on VA loans, I would refer you here: https://www.benefits.va.gov/homeloans/

And if you'd like to see whether or not you are eligible for a USDA loan, check out their website here: https://bit.ly/3uFUAwB

If you're concerned about your spouse's credit score, check out this brief article from Kiplinger, another favorite financial source of mine: https://bit.ly/3g9kvYl

And this one from Money Under 30 has more great info on the topic: https://bit.ly/2SSVlVT

For more information on how to get rid of your private mortgage insurance (PMI) early, Bankrate has a great article here: https://bit.ly/3fJJWR6

And from the Consumer Financial Protection Bureau (CFPB) themselves: https://bit.ly/3g3Kdx5

By far my favorite calculator to help you see the pros and cons of a 15-year versus 30-year loan is this one from Nerd Wallet: https://bit.ly/3wQYELH

But if you're still deciding between the two options, check out this article from Investopedia: https://bit.ly/34ErJ17

I like this calculator to play around with how much money and time will be saved by making extra payments to your mortgage. There are plenty out there, perhaps even from your mortgage servicer as well, but this one gets the job done: https://bit.ly/3i9I45T

Lastly, to get a jump on your closing cost estimates, here is a great summary: https://bit.ly/3z0pnY4

Step 7 Resources

Stumped by home inspections? Check out this resource here: https://bit.ly/3uNsvU1

Baffled by appraisals? More info here: https://bit.ly/3cemklw

Puzzled by homeowner's insurance? Investopedia has you covered again: https://bit.ly/3pfnBhj

Bewildered by title insurance? Definitely check out this article from Nerd Wallet: https://bit.ly/3wSheDf

Wandering through your final walk through? Read this first! https://bit.ly/3fZ5VCw

Perplexed by your closing disclosure? Ruminate no more! More from the CFPB: https://bit.ly/3g33sXD

Step 8 Resources

Dave Ramsey has some great information in this article about closing on a house, if you feel you still need some guidance: https://bit.ly/3gkNRmH

And finally, as far as when, exactly, you can expect to take official ownership of your home, this article has some more guidance for you: https://bit.ly/3fLhjD7

I hope that these resources have been helpful to you. With the exception of rare and specific circumstances, the contents of this book, along with these resources, should be all you need to know to go from Zero to Homeowner. I wish you many dollars saved and many headaches avoided!

REFERENCES

Better. (2021, January 22). *Home Buying Process: Step by Step Timeline: Better Mortgage.* Better Mortgage Resources. https://bit.ly/3uJbxpW.

Better Money Habits. (2021, May 11). *What Are Closing Costs and How Much Will I Pay?* Better Money Habits. https://bit.ly/3z0pnY4.

Bundrick, H. M. (2021, March 5). *How Much Down Payment Do You Need to Buy a Home?* NerdWallet. https://bit.ly/3fKZILr.

Bundrick, H. M. (n.d.). *How Much House Can I Afford?: NerdWallet: Affordability Calculator.* How Much House Can I Afford? | NerdWallet | Affordability Calculator. https://bit.ly/3yPxk2x.

Bundrick, H. M. (2017, September 18). *Title Insurance: What It Is and Why You (Probably) Need It.* NerdWallet. https://bit.ly/3wSheDf.

Extra Mortgage Payments Calculator. Extra Payment Mortgage Calculator: Making Additional Home Loan Payments. (n.d.). https://bit.ly/3i9I45T.

First Time Home Buyer Expenses You Need To Save For. First Time Home Buyer Expenses You Need To Save For | Rocket Mortgage. (n.d.). https://bit.ly/3uC9jbD.

First-Time Home Buyer Programs by State. NerdWallet. (n.d.). https://bit.ly/3fIBDoA.

Folger, J. (2021, May 25). *How Much Do Real Estate Agents Make?* Investopedia. https://bit.ly/34Ii9dq.

Harris, B. (2021, February 5). *Buying a Home in a Different State - What You Need to Know in 2021.* Tips for Buying a Home Out of State in 2021 | New American Funding. https://bit.ly/34AQCL5.

How to Improve Your FICO Score: myFICO. How to Improve Your FICO Score | myFICO | myFICO. (2018, October 19). https://bit.ly/2Tutag1.

How To Make An Offer On A House: 5 Steps. How To Make An Offer On A House: 5 Steps | Rocket Mortgage. (n.d.). https://bit.ly/3vOzoWp.

Jespersen, C. (2021, May 25). *Free Budget Spreadsheets and Templates*. NerdWallet. https://bit.ly/3g5gow8.

Kumok, Z. (n.d.). *Couples' Credit - How Credit Scores Work With Your Significant Other*. Money Under 30. https://bit.ly/2SSVlVT.

Lankford, K. (2010, December 30). *When One Spouse's Credit Score Is Lower*. Kiplinger. https://bit.ly/3g9kvYl.

Majaski, C. (2021, May 31). *15-Year vs. 30-Year Mortgage: What's the Difference?* Investopedia. https://bit.ly/34ErJ17.

Marquand, B. (2021, January 26). *How a Home Appraisal Works and How Much It Costs*. NerdWallet. https://bit.ly/3cemklw.

Marquit, M. (n.d.). *5 Types Of Mortgage Loans For Homebuyers*. Bankrate. https://bit.ly/3fMwThC.

Mercadante, K. (n.d.). *Why You Should Get A Mortgage Through A Credit Union Or Local Bank*. Money Under 30. https://bit.ly/3wNZOHP.

Miller, A. (2017, September 28). *When Do I Finally Get the Keys to My New House?* Real Estate News & Insights | realtor.com®. https://bit.ly/3fLhjD7.

Mueller, L. (2018, December 7). *How to Schedule a Home Inspection*. Moving.com. https://bit.ly/3uNsvU1.

Murray, C. (n.d.). *How Much Does A 1% Difference In Your Mortgage Rate Matter?* Money Under 30. https://bit.ly/3wVPihJ.

NerdWallet. (2021, January 28). *5 Tips for Finding the Best Mortgage Lenders.* NerdWallet. https://bit.ly/34RnwY5.

NerdWallet. (2021, February 2). *15-Year vs. 30-Year Mortgage Calculator.* NerdWallet. https://bit.ly/3wQYELH.

Nolo. (2015, March 12). *Should You Hire a Real Estate Agent or Lawyer to Buy a House?* www.nolo.com. https://bit.ly/3vJT8ue.

Ostrowski, J. (n.d.). *How To Ditch Mortgage PMI Payments.* Bankrate. https://bit.ly/3fJJWR6.

Pros and cons of different types of homes. Mortgage Rates, Mortgage News and Strategy : The Mortgage Reports. (2018, October 24). https://bit.ly/2SQ4Q8j.

Ramsey Solutions. (2021, April 20). *How to Get a Mortgage With No Credit Score.* Ramsey Solutions. https://bit.ly/3i73DDV.

Ramsey Solutions. (2021, April 26). *How Much House Can I Afford?* Ramsey Solutions. https://bit.ly/3uHTGPS.

Ramsey Solutions. (2021, March 10). *Closing on a House: What to Expect.* Ramsey Solutions. https://bit.ly/3gkNRmH.

Resources.display. (2021, May 20). *How to Improve Your Credit Score Fast*. Experian. https://bit.ly/3fGCHcJ.

Sarah. (2021, March 25). *7 of The Best Budget Templates And Tools*. Clever Girl Finance. https://bit.ly/2Tqw9WQ.

Sato, G. (2020, November 20). *Is It Better to Use a Mortgage Broker or Bank?* Experian. https://bit.ly/3ySCbjj.

Segal, T. (2021, May 24). *The Hidden Costs of Owning a Home*. Investopedia. https://bit.ly/3g32tXn.

Segal, T. (2021, March 15). *Homeowners Insurance Guide: A Beginner's Overview*. Investopedia. https://bit.ly/3pfnBhj.

Sutton, M., & says:, T. B. (2021, February 25). *Top 5 Different Types of House Styles: Pros and Cons: Homes for Heroes*. Homes for Heroes®. https://bit.ly/2TyArvw.

Tips For The Final Walkthrough Before Closing. Tips For The Final Walkthrough Before Closing | Quicken Loans. (n.d.). https://bit.ly/3fZ5VCw.

What is a Closing Disclosure? Consumer Financial Protection Bureau. (n.d.). https://bit.ly/3g33sXD.

When can I remove private mortgage insurance (PMI) from my loan? Consumer Financial Protection Bureau. (n.d.). https://bit.ly/3g3Kdx5.

Wichter January 6, Z. (n.d.). *How Much House Can I Afford?: Bankrate: New House Calculator.* Bankrate. https://bit.ly/3g3oVQe.

Wills, J. (2021, May 19). *How Do Mortgage Lenders Make Money?* Investopedia. https://bit.ly/3vS1QXG.

Made in the USA
Middletown, DE
10 July 2022